Symfony

Symfony 5: The Fast Track

Fabien Potencier

https://fabien.potencier.org/

@fabpot

@fabpot

Symfony 5: The Fast Track

ISBN-13: 978-2-918390-37-4

Symfony SAS

92-98, boulevard Victor Hugo
92 110 Clichy
France

If you find typos or errors, feel free to report them at *support@symfony.com*. This book is continuously updated based on user feedback.

Locale	en
Original English Text Version	v1.0.19
Text Translation Version	v1.0.19
Generated Code Version	5.0-4
Book Generated Date	August 10, 2020

Contents at a Glance

Table of Contents

Acknowledgments

I love books. Books that I can hold in hands.

The last time I wrote a book about Symfony was exactly 10 years ago. It was about Symfony 1.4. I have never written about Symfony since then!

I was so excited to write again about Symfony that I finished the first draft in a week. But the version you are reading took way more time. Writing a book takes a lot of time and energy. From the cover design to the page layout. From code tweaks to peer reviews. It is almost never finished. You can always improve a section, enhance some piece of code, fix some typos, or rewrite an explanation to make it shorter and better.

Writing a book is a journey that you don't want to do alone. Many people contributed directly or indirectly. Thank you all!

I want to sincerely thank all the great people who spent a lot of time reviewing the content to spot typos and improve the content; some even helped me write some of the code snippets:

Javier Eguiluz	Kévin Dunglas
Ryan Weaver	Tugdual Saunier
Titouan Galopin	Grégoire Pineau
Nicolas Grekas	Alexandre Salomé

Translators

The official Symfony documentation is only available in English. We had some translations in the past but we decided to stop providing them as they were always out of sync. And outdated documentation is probably worse than no documentation at all.

The main issue with translations is maintenance. The Symfony documentation is updated every single day by dozens of contributors. Having a team of volunteers translating all changes in near real time is almost impossible.

However, translating a book like the one you are currently reading is more manageable as I tried to write about features that won't change much over time. This is why the book contents should stay quite stable over time.

But why would we ever want non-English documentation in a tech world where English is the de facto default language? Symfony is used by developers everywhere in the world. And some of them are less comfortable reading English material. Translating some "getting started" documentation is part of the Symfony diversity initiative in which we strive to find ways to make Symfony as inclusive as possible.

As you can imagine, translating more than 300 pages is a huge amount of work, and I want to thank all the people who helped translating this book:

TRANSLATOR_LIST

Company Backers

This book has been *backed*[1] by people around the world who helped this project financially. Thanks to them, this content is available online for free and available as a paper book during Symfony conferences.

https://packagist.com/

https://darkmira.io/

https://blackfire.io/

https://basecom.de/

https://dats.team/

https://sensiolabs.com/

https://les-tilleuls.coop/

https://redant.nl/

https://www.akeneo.com/

https://www.facile.it/

https://izi-by-edf.fr/

https://www.musement.com/

https://setono.com/

---

1. `https://www.kickstarter.com/projects/fabpot/symfony-5-the-fast-track`

Individual Backers

Javier Eguiluz	⬡	@javiereguiluz
Tugdual Saunier	⬡	@tucksaun
Alexandre Salomé	⬀	https://alexandre.salome.fr
Timo Bakx	🐦	@TimoBakx
Arkadius Stefanski	⬀	https://ar.kadi.us
Oskar Stark	⬡	@OskarStark
slaubi		
Jérémy Romey	🐦	@jeremyFreeAgent
Nicolas Scolari		
Guys & Gals at SymfonyCasts	⬀	https://symfonycasts.com
Roberto santana	🐦	@robertosanval
Ismael Ambrosi	🐦	@iambrosi
Mathias STRASSER	⬀	https://roukmoute.github.io/
Platform.sh team	⬀	http://www.platform.sh
ongoing	⬀	https://www.ongoing.ch
Magnus Nordlander	⬡	@magnusnordlander
Nicolas Séverin	⬡	@nico-incubiq
Centarro	⬀	https://www.centarro.io
Lior Chamla	⬀	https://learn.web-develop.me
Art Hundiak	⬡	@ahundiak
Manuel de Ruiter	⬀	https://www.optiwise.nl/
Vincent Huck		
Jérôme Nadaud	⬀	https://nadaud.io
Michael Piecko	⬡	@mpiecko
Tobias Schilling	⬀	https://tschilling.dev
ACSEO	⬀	https://www.acseo.fr
Omines Internetbureau	⬀	https://www.omines.nl/
Seamus Byrne	⬀	http://seamusbyrne.com

Pavel Dubinin	@geekdevs
Jean-Jacques PERUZZI	https://linkedin.com/in/jjperuzzi
Alexandre Jardin	@ajardin
Christian Ducrot	http://ducrot.de
Alexandre HUON	@Aleksanthaar
François Pluchino	@francoispluchino
We Are Builders	https://we.are.builders
Rector	@rectorphp
Ilyas Salikhov	@salikhov
Romaric Drigon	@romaricdrigon
Lukáš Moravec	@morki
Malik Meyer-Heder	@mehlichmeyer
Amrouche Hamza	@cDaed
Russell Flynn	https://custard.no
Shrihari Pandit	@shriharipandit
Salma NK.	@os_rescue
Nicolas Grekas	
Roman Ihoshyn	https://ihoshyn.com
Radu Topala	https://www.trisoft.ro
Andrey Reinwald	https://www.facebook.com/andreinwald
JoliCode	@JoliCode
Rokas Mikalkėnas	
Zeljko Mitic	@strictify
Wojciech Kania	@wkania
Andrea Cristaudo	https://andrea.cristaudo.eu/
Adrien BRAULT-LESAGE	@AdrienBrault
Cristoforo Stevio Cervino	http://www.steviostudio.it
Michele Sangalli	
Florian Reiner	http://florianreiner.com

Ion Bazan		@IonBazan
Marisa Clardy		@MarisaCodes
Donatas Lomsargis		http://donatas.dev
Johnny Lattouf		@johnnylattouf
Duilio Palacios		https://styde.net
Pierre Grimaud		@pgrimaud
Marcos Labad Díaz		@esmiz
Stephan Huber		https://www.factorial.io
Loïc Vernet		https://www.strangebuzz.com
Daniel Knoch		http://www.cariba.de
Emagma		http://www.emagma.fr
Gilles Doge		
Malte Wunsch		@MalteWunsch
Jose Maria Valera Reales		@Chemaclass
Cleverway		https://cleverway.eu/
Nathan		@nutama
Abdellah EL GHAILANI		https://connect.symfony.com/profile/aelghailani
Solucionex		https://www.solucionex.com
Elnéris Dang		https://linkedin.com/in/elneris-dang/
Class Central		https://www.classcentral.com/
Ike Borup		https://idaho.dev/
Christoph Lühr		https://www.christoph-luehr.com/
Zig Websoftware		http://www.zig.nl
Dénes Fakan		@DenesFakan
Danny van Kooten		http://dvk.co
Denis Azarov		http://azarov.de
Martin Poirier T.		https://linkedin.com/in/mpoiriert/
Dmytro Feshchenko		@dmytrof
Carl Casbolt		https://www.platinumtechsolutions.co.uk/
Irontec		https://www.irontec.com

Lukas Plümper	☑ https://lukaspluemper.de/
Neil Nand	☑ https://neilnand.co.uk
Andreas Möller	☑ https://localheinz.com
Alexey Buldyk	☑ https://buldyk.pw
Page Carbajal	☑ https://pagecarbajal.com
Florian Voit	☑ https://rootsh311.de
Webmozarts GmbH	☑ https://webmozarts.com
Alexander M. Turek	☺ @derrabus
Zan Baldwin	🐦 @ZanBaldwin
Ben Marks, Magento	☑ http://bhmarks.com

Family Love

Family support is everything. A big thank-you to my wife, **Hélène** and my two wonderful children, **Thomas** and **Lucas**, for their continuous support.

Enjoy Thomas's illustration… and the book!

Step 0
What is it about?

Symfony is one of the most successful PHP projects. It is both a strong full-stack framework and a popular set of reusable components.

With version 5, the project has probably reached maturity. I can feel that everything we have done in the past 5 years come together nicely. New low-level components, high-level integrations with other software, tools helping developers improve their productivity. The developer experience has improved substantially without sacrificing flexibility. It has never been so fun to use Symfony for a project.

If you are new to Symfony, the arrival of **Symfony 5** is the right time to learn how to develop an application, step by step. This book shows developers the power of the framework and how it can improve their productivity.

If you are already a Symfony developer, you should rediscover it. The framework has evolved dramatically during the last few years and the developer experience has improved significantly. I have the feeling that many Symfony developers are still "stuck" with old habits and that they have a hard time embracing the new ways of developing applications with Symfony. I can understand some of the reasons. The pace of evolution is staggering. When working full-time on a project, developers do not have time to follow everything happening in the community. I know first hand as I would not pretend that I can follow everything myself. Far from it.

And it is not just about new ways of doing things. It is also about new components: HTTP client, Mailer, Workflow, Messenger. They are game changers. They should change the way you think about a Symfony application.

I also feel the need for a new book as the Web has evolved a lot. Topics like *APIs*[1], *SPAs*[2], *containerization*[3], *Continuous Deployment*[4], and many others should be discussed now.

Your time is precious. Don't expect long paragraphs, nor long explanations about core concepts. The book is more about the journey. Where to start. Which code to write. When. How. I will try to generate some interest on important topics and let you decide if you want to learn more and dig further.

I don't want to replicate the existing documentation either. Its quality is excellent. I will reference the documentation copiously in the "Going Further" section at the end of each step/chapter. Consider this book as a list of pointers to more resources.

The book describes the creation of an application, from scratch to production. We won't develop everything to make it production ready though. The result won't be perfect. We will take shortcuts. We might even skip some edge-case handling, validation or tests. Best practices won't be respected all the time. But we are going to touch on almost every aspect of a modern Symfony project.

While starting to work on this book, the very first thing I did was code the final application. I was impressed with the result and the velocity I was able to sustain while adding features, with very little effort. That's thanks to the documentation and the fact that Symfony 5 knows how to get out of your way. I am sure that Symfony can still be improved in many ways (and I have taken some notes about possible improvements), but the developer experience is way better than a few years ago. I want to tell the world about it.

The book is divided into steps. Each step is sub-divided into sub-steps. They should be fast to read. But more importantly, I invite you to code as you read. Write the code, test it, deploy it, tweak it.

Last, but not least, don't hesitate to ask for help if you get stuck. You might hit an edge case or a typo in the code you wrote might be difficult to find and fix. Ask questions. We have a wonderful community on *Slack*[5] and Stack Overflow.

Ready to code? Enjoy!

---

1. https://en.wikipedia.org/wiki/Application_programming_interface
2. https://en.wikipedia.org/wiki/Single-page_application
3. https://en.wikipedia.org/wiki/OS-level_virtualization
4. https://en.wikipedia.org/wiki/Continuous_deployment
5. https://symfony.com/slack

Step 1
Checking your Work Environment

Before starting to work on the project, we need to check that everyone has a good working environment. It is very important. The developers tools we have at our disposal today are very different from the ones we had 10 years ago. They have evolved a lot, for the better. It would be a shame to not leverage them. Good tools can get you a long way.

Please, don't skip this step. Or at least, read the last section about the Symfony CLI.

1.1 A Computer

You need a computer. The good news is that it can run on any popular OS: macOS, Windows, or Linux. Symfony and all the tools we are going to use are compatible with each of these.

1.2 Opinionated Choices

I want to move fast with the best options out there. I made opinionated choices for this book.

PostgreSQL[1] is going to be our choice for the database engine.

RabbitMQ[2] is the winner for queues.

1.3 IDE

You can use Notepad if you want to. I would not recommend it though.

I used to work with Textmate. Not anymore. The comfort of using a "real" IDE is priceless. Auto-completion, **use** statements added and sorted automatically, jumping from one file to another are a few features that will boost your productivity.

I would recommend using *Visual Studio Code*[3] or *PhpStorm*[4]. The former is free, the latter is not but has a better integration with Symfony (thanks to the *Symfony Support Plugin*[5]). It is up to you. I know you want to know which IDE I am using. I am writing this book in Visual Studio Code.

1.4 Terminal

We will switch from the IDE to the command line all the time. You can use your IDE's built-in terminal, but I prefer to use a real one to have more space.

Linux comes built-in with `Terminal`. Use *iTerm2*[6] on macOS. On Windows, *Hyper*[7] works well.

1.5 Git

My last book recommended Subversion for version control. It looks like everybody is using *Git*[8] now.

On Windows, install *Git bash*[9].

---

1. https://www.postgresql.org/
2. https://www.rabbitmq.com/
3. https://code.visualstudio.com/
4. https://www.jetbrains.com/phpstorm/
5. https://plugins.jetbrains.com/plugin/7219-symfony-support
6. https://iterm2.com/
7. https://hyper.is/
8. https://git-scm.com/
9. https://gitforwindows.org/

Be sure you know how to do the common operations like running `git clone`, `git log`, `git show`, `git diff`, `git checkout`, ...

1.6 PHP

We will use Docker for services, but I like to have PHP installed on my local computer for performance, stability, and simplicity reasons. Call me old school if you like, but the combination of a local PHP and Docker services is the perfect combo for me.

Use PHP 7.3 if you can, maybe 7.4 depending on when you are reading this book. Check that the following PHP extensions are installed or install them now: `intl`, `pdo_pgsql`, `xsl`, `amqp`, `gd`, `openssl`, `sodium`. Optionally install `redis` and `curl` as well.

You can check the extensions currently enabled via `php -m`.

We also need `php-fpm` if your platform supports it, `php-cgi` works as well.

1.7 Composer

Managing dependencies is everything nowadays with a Symfony project. Get the latest version of *Composer*[10], the package management tool for PHP.

If you are not familiar with Composer, take some time to read about it.

 You don't need to type the full command names: `composer req` does the same as `composer require`, use `composer rem` instead of `composer remove`, ...

1.8 Docker and Docker Compose

Services are going to be managed by Docker and Docker Compose. *Install them*[11] and start Docker. If you are a first time user, get familiar with the tool. Don't panic though, our usage will be very straightforward. No fancy configurations, no complex setup.

---

10. https://getcomposer.org/
11. https://docs.docker.com/install/

1.9 Symfony CLI

Last, but not least, we will use the symfony CLI to boost our productivity. From the local web server it provides, to full Docker integration and SymfonyCloud support, it will be a great time saver.

Install the *Symfony CLI*[12] and move it under your $PATH. Create a *SymfonyConnect*[13] account if you don't have one already and log in via symfony login.

To use HTTPS locally, we also need to *install a CA*[14] to enable TLS support. Run the following command:

```
$ symfony server:ca:install
```

Check that your computer has all needed requirements by running the following command:

```
$ symfony book:check-requirements
```

If you want to get fancy, you can also run the *Symfony proxy*[15]. It is optional but it allows you to get a local domain name ending with .wip for your project.

When executing a command in a terminal, we will almost always prefix it with symfony like in symfony composer instead of just composer, or symfony console instead of ./bin/console.

The main reason is that the Symfony CLI automatically sets some environment variables based on the services running on your machine via Docker. These environment variables are available for HTTP requests because the local web server injects them automatically. So, using symfony on the CLI ensures that you have the same behavior across the board.

Moreover, the Symfony CLI automatically selects the "best" possible PHP version for the project.

---

12. https://symfony.com/download
13. https://connect.symfony.com/
14. https://symfony.com/doc/current/setup/symfony_server.html#enabling-tls
15. https://symfony.com/doc/current/setup/symfony_server.html#setting-up-the-local-proxy

Step 2
Introducing the Project

We need to find a project to work on. It is quite a challenge as we need to find a project large enough to cover Symfony thoroughly, but at the same time, it should be small enough; I don't want you to get bored implementing similar features more than once.

2.1 Revealing the Project

As the book has to be released during SymfonyCon Amsterdam, it might be nice if the project is somehow related to Symfony and conferences. What about a *guestbook*[1]? A livre d'or as we say in French. I like the old-fashioned and outdated feeling of developing a guestbook in 2019!

We have it. The project is all about getting feedback on conferences: a list of conferences on the homepage, a page for each conference, full of nice comments. A comment is composed of some small text and an optional photo taken during the conference. I suppose I have just written down all the specifications we need to get started.

The *project* will contain several *applications*. A traditional web application with an HTML frontend, an API, and an SPA for mobile phones. How does that sound?

---

1. https://en.wikipedia.org/wiki/Guestbook

2.2 Learning is Doing

Learning is doing. Period. Reading a book about Symfony is nice. Coding an application on your personal computer while reading a book about Symfony is even better. This book is very special as everything has been done to let you follow along, code, and be sure to get the same results as I had locally on my machine when I coded it initially.

The book contains all the code you need to write and all the commands you need to execute to get the final result. No code is missing. All commands are written down. This is possible because modern Symfony applications have very little boilerplate code. Most of the code we will write together is about the project's *business logic*. Everything else is mostly automated or generated automatically for us.

2.3 Looking at the Final Infrastructure Diagram

Even if the project idea seems simple, we are not going to build an "Hello World"-like project. We won't only use PHP and a database.

The goal is to create a project with some of the complexities you might find in real-life. Want a proof? Have a look at the final infrastructure of the project:

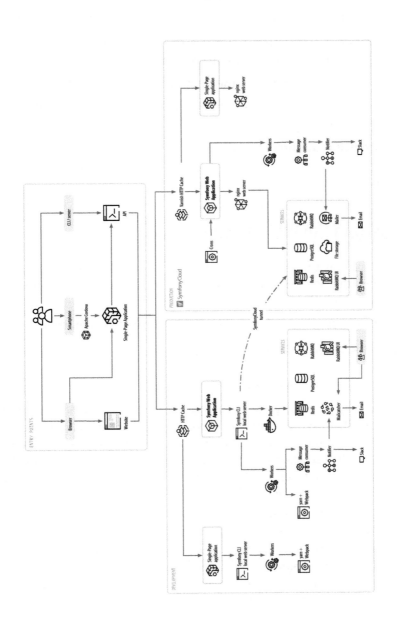

One of the great benefit of using a framework is the small amount of code needed to develop such a project:

- 20 PHP classes under `src/` for the website;
- 550 PHP Logical Lines of Code (LLOC) as reported by *PHPLOC*[2];
- 40 lines of configuration tweaks in 3 files (via annotations and YAML), mainly to configure the backend design;
- 20 lines of development infrastructure configuration (Docker);
- 100 lines of production infrastructure configuration (SymfonyCloud);
- 5 explicit environment variables.

Ready for the challenge?

2.4 Getting the Project Source Code

To continue on the old-fashioned theme, I could have created a CD containing the source code, right? But what about a Git repository companion instead?

Clone the *guestbook repository*[3] somewhere on your local machine:

```
$ symfony new --version=5.0-4 --book guestbook
```

This repository contains all the code of the book.

Note that we are using `symfony new` instead of `git clone` as the command does more than just cloning the repository (hosted on Github under the `the-fast-track` organization: `https://github.com/the-fast-track/book-5.0-4`). It also starts the web server, the containers, migrates the database, loads fixtures, ... After running the command, the website should be up and running, ready to be used.

The code is 100% guaranteed to be synchronized with the code in the book (use the exact repository URL listed above). Trying to manually synchronize changes from the book with the source code in the repository is almost impossible. I tried in the past. I failed. It is just impossible. Especially for books like the ones I write: books that tells you a story about developing a website. As each chapter depends on the previous ones, a change might have consequences in all following

---

2. `https://github.com/sebastianbergmann/phploc`
3. `https://github.com/the-fast-track/book-5.0-4`

chapters.

The good news is that the Git repository for this book is *automatically generated* from the book content. You read that right. I like to automate everything, so there is a script whose job is to read the book and create the Git repository. There is a nice side-effect: when updating the book, the script will fail if the changes are inconsistent or if I forget to update some instructions. That's BDD, Book Driven Development!

2.5 Navigating the Source Code

Even better, the repository is not just about the final version of the code on the `master` branch. The script executes each action explained in the book and it commits its work at the end of each section. It also tags each step and substep to ease browsing the code. Nice, isn't it?

If you are lazy, you can get the state of the code at the end of a step by checking out the right tag. For instance, if you'd like to read and test the code at the end of step 10, execute the following:

```
$ symfony book:checkout 10
```

Like for cloning the repository, we are not using `git checkout` but `symfony book:checkout`. The command ensures that whatever the state you are currently in, you end up with a functional website for the step you ask for. **Be warned that all data, code, and containers are removed by this operation.**

You can also check out any substep:

```
$ symfony book:checkout 10.2
```

Again, I highly recommend you code yourself. But if you get stuck, you can always compare what you have with the content of the book.

Not sure that you got everything right in substep 10.2? Get the diff:

```
$ git diff step-10-1...step-10-2

# And for the very first substep of a step:
$ git diff step-9...step-10-1
```

Want to know when a file has been created or modified?

```
$ git log -- src/Controller/ConferenceController.php
```

You can also browse diffs, tags, and commits directly on GitHub. This is a great way to copy/paste code if you are reading a paper book!

Step 3
Going from Zero to Production

I like to go fast. I want our little project to be live as fast as possible. Like now. In production. As we haven't developed anything yet, we will start by deploying a nice and simple "Under construction" page. You will love it!

Spend some time trying to find the ideal, old fashioned, and animated "Under construction" GIF on the Internet. Here is *the one*[1] I'm going to use:

---

1. http://clipartmag.com/images/website-under-construction-image-6.gif

I told you, it is going to be a lot of fun.

3.1 Initializing the Project

Create a new Symfony project with the `symfony` CLI tool we have previously installed together:

```
$ symfony new guestbook --version=5.0
$ cd guestbook
```

This command is a thin wrapper on top of `Composer` that eases the creation of Symfony projects. It uses a *project skeleton*[2] that includes the bare minimum dependencies; the Symfony components that are needed for almost any project: a console tool and the HTTP abstraction needed to create Web applications.

If you have a look at the GitHub repository for the skeleton, you will notice that it is almost empty. Just a `composer.json` file. But the `guestbook` directory is full of files. How is that even possible? The answer lies in the `symfony/flex` package. Symfony Flex is a Composer plugin that hooks into the installation process. When it detects a package for which it has a *recipe*, it executes it.

The main entry point of a Symfony Recipe is a manifest file that describes the operations that need to be done to automatically register the package in a Symfony application. You never have to read a README file to install a package with Symfony. Automation is a key feature of Symfony.

As Git is installed on our machine, `symfony new` also created a Git repository for us and it added the very first commit.

Have a look at the directory structure:

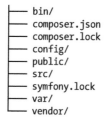
```
├── bin/
├── composer.json
├── composer.lock
├── config/
├── public/
├── src/
├── symfony.lock
├── var/
└── vendor/
```

The `bin/` directory contains the main CLI entry point: `console`. You will use it all the time.

---

2. https://github.com/symfony/skeleton

The `config/` directory is made of a set of default and sensible configuration files. One file per package. You will barely change them, trusting the defaults is almost always a good idea.

The `public/` directory is the web root directory, and the `index.php` script is the main entry point for all dynamic HTTP resources.

The `src/` directory hosts all the code you will write; that's where you will spend most of your time. By default, all classes under this directory use the `App` PHP namespace. It is your home. Your code. Your domain logic. Symfony has very little to say there.

The `var/` directory contains caches, logs, and files generated at runtime by the application. You can leave it alone. It is the only directory that needs to be writable in production.

The `vendor/` directory contains all packages installed by Composer, including Symfony itself. That's our secret weapon to be more productive. Let's not reinvent the wheel. You will rely on existing libraries to do the hard work. The directory is managed by Composer. Never touch it.

That's all you need to know for now.

3.2 Creating some Public Resources

Anything under `public/` is accessible via a browser. For instance, if you move your animated GIF file (name it `under-construction.gif`) into a new `public/images/` directory, it will be available at a URL like `https://localhost/images/under-construction.gif`.

Download my GIF image here:

```
$ mkdir public/images/
$ php -r "copy('http://clipartmag.com/images/website-under-construction-
image-6.gif', 'public/images/under-construction.gif');"
```

3.3 Launching a Local Web Server

The `symfony` CLI comes with a Web Server that is optimized for development work. You won't be surprised if I tell you that it works nicely with Symfony. Never use it in production though.

From the project directory, start the web server in the background (`-d` flag):

```
$ symfony server:start -d
```

The server started on the first available port, starting with 8000. As a shortcut, open the website in a browser from the CLI:

```
$ symfony open:local
```

Your favorite browser should take the focus and open a new tab that displays something similar to the following:

 To troubleshoot problems, run symfony server:log; it tails the logs from the web server, PHP, and your application.

Browse to /images/under-construction.gif. Does it look like this?

Satisfied? Let's commit our work:

```
$ git add public/images
```

```
$ git commit -m'Add the under construction image'
```

3.4 Adding a favicon

To avoid being "spammed" by 404 HTTP errors in the logs because of a missing favicon requested by browsers, let's add one now:

```
$ php -r "copy('https://symfony.com/favicon.ico', 'public/favicon.ico');"
$ git add public/
$ git commit -m'Add a favicon'
```

3.5 Preparing for Production

What about deploying our work to production? I know, we don't even have a proper HTML page yet to welcome our users. But being able to see the little "under construction" image on a production server would be a great step forward. And you know the motto: *deploy early and often*.

You can host this application on any provider supporting PHP... which means almost all hosting providers out there. Check a few things though: we want the latest PHP version and the possibility to host services like a database, a queue, and some more.

I have made my choice, it's going to be *SymfonyCloud*[3]. It provides everything we need and it helps fund the development of Symfony.

The symfony CLI has built-in support for SymfonyCloud. Let's initialize a SymfonyCloud project:

```
$ symfony project:init
```

This command creates a few files needed by SymfonyCloud, namely .symfony/services.yaml, .symfony/routes.yaml, and .symfony.cloud.yaml.

Add them to Git and commit:

```
$ git add .
$ git commit -m"Add SymfonyCloud configuration"
```

---

3. https://symfony.com/cloud

Using the generic and dangerous `git add .` works fine as a `.gitignore` file has been generated that automatically excludes all files we don't want to commit.

3.6 Going to Production

Deploy time?

Create a new SymfonyCloud Project:

```
$ symfony project:create --title="Guestbook" --plan=development
```

This command does a lot:

- The first time you launch this command, authenticate with your SymfonyConnect credentials if not done already.

- It provisions a new project on SymfonyCloud (you get 7 days *for free* on any new development project).

Then, deploy:

```
$ symfony deploy
```

The code is deployed by pushing the Git repository. At the end of the command, the project will have a specific domain name you can use to access it.

Check that everything worked fine:

```
$ symfony open:remote
```

You should get a 404, but browsing to `/images/under-construction.gif` should reveal our work.

Note that you don't get the beautiful default Symfony page on SymfonyCloud. Why? You will learn soon that Symfony supports several environments and SymfonyCloud automatically deployed the code in the production environment.

 If you want to delete the project on SymfonyCloud, use the `project:delete` command.

Going Further

- The *Symfony Recipes Server*[4], where you can find all the available recipes for your Symfony applications;
- The repositories for the *official Symfony recipes*[5] and for the *recipes contributed by the community*[6], where you can submit your own recipes;
- The *Symfony Local Web Server*[7];
- The *SymfonyCloud documentation*[8].

---

4. https://flex.symfony.com/
5. https://github.com/symfony/recipes
6. https://github.com/symfony/recipes-contrib
7. https://symfony.com/doc/current/setup/symfony_server.html
8. https://symfony.com/doc/cloud

Step 4
Adopting a Methodology

Teaching is about repeating the same thing again and again. I won't do that. I promise. At the end of each step, you should do a little dance and save your work. It is like `Ctrl+S` but for a website.

4.1 Implementing a Git Strategy

At the end of each step, don't forget to commit your changes:

```
$ git add .
$ git commit -m'Add some new feature'
```

You can safely add "everything" as Symfony manages a `.gitignore` file for you. And each package can add more configuration. Have a look at the current content:

```
.gitignore
###> symfony/framework-bundle ###
/.env.local
/.env.local.php
/.env.*.local
/public/bundles/
/var/
/vendor/
###< symfony/framework-bundle ###
```

The funny strings are markers added by Symfony Flex so that it knows what to remove if you decide to uninstall a dependency. I told you, all the tedious work is done by Symfony, not you.

It could be nice to push your repository to a server somewhere. GitHub, GitLab, or Bitbucket are good choices.

If you are deploying on SymfonyCloud, you already have a copy of the Git repository, but you should not rely on it. It is only for deployment usage. It is not a backup.

4.2 Deploying to Production Continuously

Another good habit is to deploy frequently. Deploying at the end of each step is a good pace:

```
$ symfony deploy
```

Step 5
Troubleshooting Problems

Setting up a project is also about having the right tools to debug problems.

5.1 Installing more Dependencies

Remember that the project was created with very few dependencies. No template engine. No debug tools. No logging system. The idea is that you can add more dependencies whenever you need them. Why would you depend on a template engine if you develop an HTTP API or a CLI tool?

How can we add more dependencies? Via Composer. Besides "regular" Composer packages, we will work with two "special" kinds of packages:

- *Symfony Components*: Packages that implement core features and low level abstractions that most applications need (routing, console, HTTP client, mailer, cache, ...);

- *Symfony Bundles*: Packages that add high-level features or provide integrations with third-party libraries (bundles are mostly contributed by the community).

To begin with, let's add the Symfony Profiler, a time saver when you need to find the root cause of a problem:

```
$ symfony composer req profiler --dev
```

`profiler` is an alias for the `symfony/profiler-pack` package.

Aliases are not a Composer feature, but a concept provided by Symfony to make your life easier. Aliases are shortcuts for popular Composer packages. Want an ORM for your application? Require `orm`. Want to develop an API? Require `api`. These aliases are automatically resolved to one or more regular Composer packages. They are opinionated choices made by the Symfony core team.

Another neat feature is that you can always omit the `symfony` vendor. Require `cache` instead of `symfony/cache`.

 Do you remember that we mentioned a Composer plugin named `symfony/flex` before? Aliases are one of its features.

5.2 Understanding Symfony Environments

Did you notice the `--dev` flag on the `composer req` command? As the Symfony Profiler is only useful during development, we want to avoid it being installed in production.

Symfony supports the notion of *environments*. By default, it has built-in support for three, but you can add as many as you like: `dev`, `prod`, and `test`. All environments share the same code, but they represent different *configurations*.

For instance, all debugging tools are enabled in the `dev` environment. In the `prod` one, the application is optimized for performance.

Switching from one environment to another can be done by changing the `APP_ENV` environment variable.

When you deployed to SymfonyCloud, the environment (stored in `APP_ENV`) was automatically switched to `prod`.

5.3 Managing Environment Configurations

`APP_ENV` can be set by using "real" environment variables in your terminal:

```
$ export APP_ENV=dev
```

Using real environment variables is the preferred way to set values like `APP_ENV` on production servers. But on development machines, having to define many environment variables can be cumbersome. Instead, define them in a .env file.

A sensible .env file was generated automatically for you when the project was created:

```
.env
###> symfony/framework-bundle ###
APP_ENV=dev
APP_SECRET=c2927f273163f7225a358e3a1bbbed8a
#TRUSTED_PROXIES=127.0.0.1,127.0.0.2
#TRUSTED_HOSTS='^localhost|example\.com$'
###< symfony/framework-bundle ###
```

 Any package can add more environment variables to this file thanks to their recipe used by Symfony Flex.

The .env file is committed to the repository and describes the *default* values from production. You can override these values by creating a .env.local file. This file should not be committed and that's why the .gitignore file is already ignoring it.

Never store secret or sensitive values in these files. We will see how to manage secrets in another step.

5.4 Logging all the Things

Out of the box, logging and debugging capabilities are limited on new projects. Let's add more tools to help us investigate issues in development, but also in production:

```
$ symfony composer req logger
```

For debugging tools, let's only install them in development:

```
$ symfony composer req debug --dev
```

5.5 Discovering the Symfony Debugging Tools

If you refresh the homepage, you should now see a toolbar at the bottom of the screen:

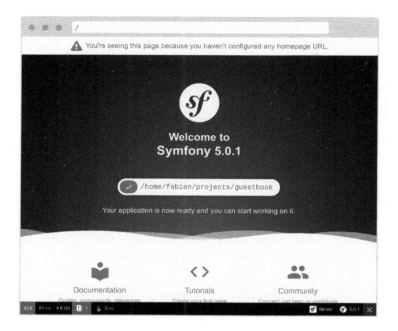

The first thing you might notice is the **404** in red. Remember that this page is a placeholder as we have not defined a homepage yet. Even if the default page that welcomes you is beautiful, it is still an error page. So the correct HTTP status code is 404, not 200. Thanks to the web debug toolbar, you have the information right away.

If you click on the small exclamation point, you get the "real" exception message as part of the logs in the Symfony profiler. If you want to see the stack trace, click on the "Exception" link on the left menu.

Whenever there is an issue with your code, you will see an exception page like the following that gives you everything you need to understand the issue and where it comes from:

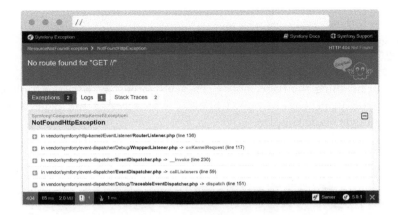

Take some time to explore the information inside the Symfony profiler by clicking around.

Logs are also quite useful in debugging sessions. Symfony has a convenient command to tail all the logs (from the web server, PHP, and your application):

```
$ symfony server:log
```

Let's do a small experiment. Open `public/index.php` and break the PHP code there (add foobar in the middle of the code for instance). Refresh the page in the browser and observe the log stream:

```
Dec 21 10:04:59 |DEBUG| PHP    PHP Parse error:  syntax error, unexpected
'use' (T_USE) in public/index.php on line 5 path="/usr/bin/php7.42"
php="7.42.0"
Dec 21 10:04:59 |ERROR| SERVER GET  (500) / ip="127.0.0.1"
```

The output is beautifully colored to get your attention on errors.

Another great debug helper is the Symfony `dump()` function. It is always available and allows you to dump complex variables in a nice and interactive format.

Temporarily change `public/index.php` to dump the Request object:

```
--- a/public/index.php
+++ b/public/index.php
@@ -23,5 +23,8 @@ if ($trustedHosts = $_SERVER['TRUSTED_HOSTS'] ??
$_ENV['TRUSTED_HOSTS'] ?? false
 $kernel = new Kernel($_SERVER['APP_ENV'], (bool) $_SERVER['APP_DEBUG']);
 $request = Request::createFromGlobals();
 $response = $kernel->handle($request);
+
+dump($request);
```

```
+    $response->send();
     $kernel->terminate($request, $response);
```

When refreshing the page, notice the new "target" icon in the toolbar; it lets you inspect the dump. Click on it to access a full page where navigating is made simpler:

Revert the changes before committing the other changes done in this step:

```
$ git checkout public/index.php
```

5.6 Configuring your IDE

In the development environment, when an exception is thrown, Symfony displays a page with the exception message and its stack trace. When displaying a file path, it adds a link that opens the file at the right line in your favorite IDE. To benefit from this feature, you need to configure your IDE. Symfony supports many IDEs out of the box; I'm using Visual Studio Code for this project:

```
--- a/config/packages/framework.yaml
+++ b/config/packages/framework.yaml
@@ -14,3 +14,5 @@ framework:
     #fragments: true
```

```
php_errors:
    log: true
+
+   ide: vscode
```

Linked files are not limited to exceptions. For instance, the controller in
the web debug toolbar becomes clickable after configuring the IDE.

5.7 Debugging Production

Debugging production servers is always trickier. You don't have access
to the Symfony profiler for instance. Logs are less verbose. But tailing the
logs is possible:

```
$ symfony logs
```

You can even connect via SSH on the web container:

```
$ symfony ssh
```

Don't worry, you cannot break anything easily. Most of the filesystem is
read-only. You won't be able to do a hot fix in production. But you will
learn a much better way later in the book.

 Going Further

- *SymfonyCasts Environments and Config Files tutorial*[1];
- *SymfonyCasts Environment Variables tutorial*[2];
- *SymfonyCasts Web Debug Toolbar and Profiler tutorial*[3];
- *Managing multiple .env files*[4] in Symfony applications.

1. https://symfonycasts.com/screencast/symfony-fundamentals/environment-config-files
2. https://symfonycasts.com/screencast/symfony-fundamentals/environment-variables
3. https://symfonycasts.com/screencast/symfony/debug-toolbar-profiler
4. https://symfony.com/doc/current/configuration.html#managing-multiple-env-files

Step 6
Creating a Controller

Our guestbook project is already live on production servers but we cheated a little bit. The project doesn't have any web pages yet. The homepage is served as a boring 404 error page. Let's fix that.

When an HTTP request comes in, like for the homepage (http://localhost:8000/), Symfony tries to find a *route* that matches the *request path* (/ here). A *route* is the link between the request path and a *PHP callable*, a function that creates the HTTP *response* for that request.

These callables are called "controllers". In Symfony, most controllers are implemented as PHP classes. You can create such a class manually, but because we like to go fast, let's see how Symfony can help us.

6.1 Being Lazy with the Maker Bundle

To generate controllers effortlessly, we can use the `symfony/maker-bundle` package:

```
$ symfony composer req maker --dev
```

As the maker bundle is only useful during development, don't forget to add the `--dev` flag to avoid it being enabled in production.

The maker bundle helps you generate a lot of different classes. We will use it all the time in this book. Each "generator" is defined in a command and all commands are part of the `make` command namespace.

The Symfony Console built-in `list` command lists all commands available under a given namespace; use it to discover all generators provided by the maker bundle:

```
$ symfony console list make
```

6.2 Choosing a Configuration Format

Before creating the first controller of the project, we need to decide on the configuration formats we want to use. Symfony supports YAML, XML, PHP, and annotations out of the box.

For *configuration related to packages*, YAML is the best choice. This is the format used in the `config/` directory. Often, when you install a new package, that package's recipe will add a new file ending in `.yaml` to that directory.

For *configuration related to PHP code*, *annotations* are a better choice as they are defined next to the code. Let me explain with an example. When a request comes in, some configuration needs to tell Symfony that the request path should be handled by a specific controller (a PHP class). When using YAML, XML or PHP configuration formats, two files are involved (the configuration file and the PHP controller file). When using annotations, the configuration is done directly in the controller class.

To manage annotations, we need to add another dependency:

```
$ symfony composer req annotations
```

You might wonder how you can guess the package name you need to install for a feature? Most of the time, you don't need to know. In many cases, Symfony contains the package to install in its error messages. Running `symfony make:controller` without the `annotations` package for instance would have ended with an exception containing a hint about installing the right package.

6.3 Generating a Controller

Create your first *Controller* via the `make:controller` command:

```
$ symfony console make:controller ConferenceController
```

The command creates a `ConferenceController` class under the `src/`

Controller/ directory. The generated class consists of some boilerplate code ready to be fine-tuned:

src/Controller/ConferenceController.php
```php
namespace App\Controller;

use Symfony\Bundle\FrameworkBundle\Controller\AbstractController;
use Symfony\Component\HttpFoundation\Response;
use Symfony\Component\Routing\Annotation\Route;

class ConferenceController extends AbstractController
{
    /**
     * @Route("/conference", name="conference")
     */
    public function index()
    {
        return $this->render('conference/index.html.twig', [
            'controller_name' => 'ConferenceController',
        ]);
    }
}
```

The `@Route("/conference", name="conference")` annotation is what makes the `index()` method a controller (the configuration is next to the code that it configures).

When you hit `/conference` in a browser, the controller is executed and a response is returned.

Tweak the route to make it match the homepage:

```diff
--- a/src/Controller/ConferenceController.php
+++ b/src/Controller/ConferenceController.php
@@ -8,7 +8,7 @@ use Symfony\Component\Routing\Annotation\Route;
 class ConferenceController extends AbstractController
 {
     /**
-     * @Route("/conference", name="conference")
+     * @Route("/", name="homepage")
     */
     public function index()
     {
```

The route `name` will be useful when we want to reference the homepage in the code. Instead of hard-coding the / path, we will use the route name.

Instead of the default rendered page, let's return a simple HTML one:

```diff
--- a/src/Controller/ConferenceController.php
+++ b/src/Controller/ConferenceController.php
@@ -3,6 +3,7 @@
 namespace App\Controller;
```

```
 use Symfony\Bundle\FrameworkBundle\Controller\AbstractController;
+use Symfony\Component\HttpFoundation\Response;
 use Symfony\Component\Routing\Annotation\Route;

 class ConferenceController extends AbstractController
@@ -12,8 +13,13 @@ class ConferenceController extends AbstractController
      */
     public function index()
     {
-        return $this->render('conference/index.html.twig', [
-            'controller_name' => 'ConferenceController',
-        ]);
+        return new Response(<<<EOF
+<html>
+    <body>
+        <img src="/images/under-construction.gif" />
+    </body>
+</html>
+EOF
+        );
     }
 }
```

Refresh the browser:

The main responsibility of a controller is to return an HTTP Response for the request.

6.4 Adding an Easter Egg

To demonstrate how a response can leverage information from the request, let's add a small *Easter egg*[1]. Whenever the homepage contains a query string like ?hello=Fabien, let's add some text to greet the person:

```
--- a/src/Controller/ConferenceController.php
```

---

1. https://en.wikipedia.org/wiki/Easter_egg_(media)#In_computing

```
+++ b/src/Controller/ConferenceController.php
@@ -3,6 +3,7 @@
 namespace App\Controller;

 use Symfony\Bundle\FrameworkBundle\Controller\AbstractController;
+use Symfony\Component\HttpFoundation\Request;
 use Symfony\Component\HttpFoundation\Response;
 use Symfony\Component\Routing\Annotation\Route;

@@ -11,11 +12,17 @@ class ConferenceController extends AbstractController
     /**
      * @Route("/", name="homepage")
      */
-    public function index()
+    public function index(Request $request)
     {
+        $greet = '';
+        if ($name = $request->query->get('hello')) {
+            $greet = sprintf('<h1>Hello %s!</h1>', htmlspecialchars($name));
+        }
+
         return new Response(<<<EOF
 <html>
     <body>
+        $greet
         <img src="/images/under-construction.gif" />
     </body>
 </html>
```

Symfony exposes the request data through a `Request` object. When
Symfony sees a controller argument with this type-hint, it automatically
knows to pass it to you. We can use it to get the `name` item from the query
string and add an `<h1>` title.

Try hitting `/` then `/?hello=Fabien` in a browser to see the difference.

 Notice the call to `htmlspecialchars()` to avoid XSS issues. This is
something that will be done automatically for us when we switch
to a proper template engine.

We could also have made the name part of the URL:

```
--- a/src/Controller/ConferenceController.php
+++ b/src/Controller/ConferenceController.php
@@ -9,13 +9,19 @@ use Symfony\Component\Routing\Annotation\Route;
 class ConferenceController extends AbstractController
 {
     /**
-     * @Route("/", name="homepage")
+     * @Route("/hello/{name}", name="homepage")
      */
-    public function index()
```

```
+    public function index(string $name = '')
     {
+        $greet = '';
+        if ($name) {
+            $greet = sprintf('<h1>Hello %s!</h1>', htmlspecialchars($name));
+        }
+
         return new Response(<<<EOF
  <html>
      <body>
+         $greet
          <img src="/images/under-construction.gif" />
      </body>
  </html>
```

The {name} part of the route is a dynamic *route parameter* - it works like a
wildcard. You can now hit /hello then /hello/Fabien in a browser to get
the same results as before. You can get the *value* of the {name} parameter
by adding a controller argument with the same *name*. So, $name.

 Going Further

- The Symfony *Routing*[2] system;

- *SymfonyCasts Routes, Controllers & Pages tutorial*[3];

- *Annotations*[4] in PHP;

- The *HttpFoundation*[5] component;

- *XSS (Cross-Site Scripting)*[6] security attacks;

- The *Symfony Routing Cheat Sheet*[7].

---

2. https://symfony.com/doc/current/routing.html
3. https://symfonycasts.com/screencast/symfony/route-controller
4. https://www.doctrine-project.org/projects/doctrine-annotations/en/1.6/annotations.html
5. https://symfony.com/doc/current/components/http_foundation.html
6. https://owasp.org/www-community/attacks/xss/
7. https://github.com/andreia/symfony-cheat-sheets/blob/master/Symfony4/routing_en_part1.pdf

Step 7
Setting up a Database

The Conference Guestbook website is about gathering feedback during conferences. We need to store the comments contributed by the conference attendees in a permanent storage.

A comment is best described by a fixed data structure: an author, their email, the text of the feedback, and an optional photo. The kind of data that can be best stored in a traditional relational database engine.

PostgreSQL is the database engine we will use.

7.1 Adding PostgreSQL to Docker Compose

On our local machine, we have decided to use Docker to manage services. Create a `docker-compose.yaml` file and add PostgreSQL as a service:

docker-compose.yaml
```yaml
version: '3'

services:
    database:
        image: postgres:11-alpine
        environment:
            POSTGRES_USER: main
            POSTGRES_PASSWORD: main
            POSTGRES_DB: main
        ports: [5432]
```

This will install a PostgreSQL server at version 11 and configure some environment variables that control the database name and credentials. The values do not really matter.

We also expose the PostgreSQL port (5432) of the container to the local host. That will help us access the database from our machine.

 The pdo_pgsql extension should have been installed when PHP was set up in a previous step.

7.2 Starting Docker Compose

Start Docker Compose in the background (-d):

```
$ docker-compose up -d
```

Wait a bit to let the database start up and check that everything is running fine:

```
$ docker-compose ps
```

Name	Command	State	Ports
guestbook_database_1	docker-entrypoint.sh postgres	Up	0.0.0.0:32780->5432/tcp

If there are no running containers or if the State column does not read Up, check the Docker Compose logs:

```
$ docker-compose logs
```

7.3 Accessing the Local Database

Using the psql command-line utility might prove useful from time to time. But you need to remember the credentials and the database name. Less obvious, you also need to know the local port the database runs on the host. Docker chooses a random port so that you can work on more than one project using PostgreSQL at the same time (the local port is part of the output of docker-compose ps).

If you run psql via the Symfony CLI, you don't need to remember anything.

The Symfony CLI automatically detects the Docker services running for

60

the project and exposes the environment variables that `psql` needs to connect to the database.

Thanks to these conventions, accessing the database via `symfony run` is much easier:

```
$ symfony run psql
```

 If you don't have the `psql` binary on your local host, you can also run it via `docker`:

```
$ docker exec -it guestbook_database_1 psql -U main -W main
```

7.4 Adding PostgreSQL to SymfonyCloud

For the production infrastructure on SymfonyCloud, adding a service like PostgreSQL should be done in the currently empty `.symfony/services.yaml` file:

.symfony/services.yaml
```
db:
    type: postgresql:11
    disk: 1024
    size: S
```

The `db` service is a PostgreSQL database at version 11 (like for Docker) that we want to provision on a small container with 1GB of disk.

We also need to "link" the DB to the application container, which is described in `.symfony.cloud.yaml`:

.symfony.cloud.yaml
```
relationships:
    database: "db:postgresql"
```

The `db` service of type `postgresql` is referenced as `database` on the application container.

The last step is to add the `pdo_pgsql` extension to the PHP runtime:

.symfony.cloud.yaml
```
runtime:
    extensions:
        - pdo_pgsql
```

```
                # other extensions here
```

Here is the full diff for the `.symfony.cloud.yaml` changes:

```
--- a/.symfony.cloud.yaml
+++ b/.symfony.cloud.yaml
@@ -4,6 +4,7 @@ type: php:7.3

 runtime:
     extensions:
+        - pdo_pgsql
        - apcu
        - mbstring
        - sodium
@@ -12,6 +13,9 @@ runtime:
 build:
     flavor: none

+relationships:
+    database: "db:postgresql"
+
 web:
     locations:
        "/":
```

Commit these changes and then re-deploy to SymfonyCloud:

```
$ git add .
$ git commit -m'Configuring the database'
$ symfony deploy
```

7.5 Accessing the SymfonyCloud Database

PostgreSQL is now running both locally via Docker and in production on SymfonyCloud.

As we have just seen, running `symfony run psql` automatically connects to the database hosted by Docker thanks to environment variables exposed by `symfony run`.

If you want to connect to PostgreSQL hosted on the production containers, you can open an SSH tunnel between the local machine and the SymfonyCloud infrastructure:

```
$ symfony tunnel:open --expose-env-vars
```

By default, SymfonyCloud services are not exposed as environment variables on the local machine. You must explicitly do so by using the --

expose-env-vars flag. Why? Connecting to the production database is a dangerous operation. You can mess with *real* data. Requiring the flag is how you confirm that this *is* what you want to do.

Now, connect to the remote PostgreSQL database via `symfony run psql` as before:

```
$ symfony run psql
```

When done, don't forget to close the tunnel:

```
$ symfony tunnel:close
```

 To run some SQL queries on the production database instead of getting a shell, you can also use the `symfony sql` command.

7.6 Exposing Environment Variables

Docker Compose and SymfonyCloud work seamlessly with Symfony thanks to environment variables.

Check all environment variables exposed by `symfony` by executing `symfony var:export`:

```
$ symfony var:export

PGHOST=127.0.0.1
PGPORT=32781
PGDATABASE=main
PGUSER=main
PGPASSWORD=main
# ...
```

The `PG*` environment variables are read by the `psql` utility. What about the others?

When a tunnel is open to SymfonyCloud with the `--expose-env-vars` flag set, the `var:export` command returns remote environment variables:

```
$ symfony tunnel:open --expose-env-vars
$ symfony var:export
$ symfony tunnel:close
```

Going Further

- *SymfonyCloud services*[1];
- *SymfonyCloud tunnel*[2];
- *PostgreSQL documentation*[3];
- *docker-compose commands*[4].

---

1. https://symfony.com/doc/master/cloud/services/intro.html#available-services
2. https://symfony.com/doc/master/cloud/services/intro.html#connecting-to-a-service
3. https://www.postgresql.org/docs/
4. https://docs.docker.com/compose/reference/

Step 8
Describing the Data Structure

To deal with the database from PHP, we are going to depend on *Doctrine*[1], a set of libraries that help developers manage databases:

```
$ symfony composer req orm
```

This command installs a few dependencies: Doctrine DBAL (a database abstraction layer), Doctrine ORM (a library to manipulate our database content using PHP objects), and Doctrine Migrations.

8.1 Configuring Doctrine ORM

How does Doctrine know the database connection? Doctrine's recipe added a configuration file, `config/packages/doctrine.yaml`, that controls its behavior. The main setting is the *database DSN*, a string containing all the information about the connection: credentials, host, port, etc. By default, Doctrine looks for a `DATABASE_URL` environment variable.

---

1. https://www.doctrine-project.org/

8.2 Understanding Symfony Environment Variable Conventions

You can define the DATABASE_URL manually in the .env or .env.local file. In fact, thanks to the package's recipe, you'll see an example DATABASE_URL in your .env file. But because the local port to PostgreSQL exposed by Docker can change, it is quite cumbersome. There is a better way.

Instead of hard-coding DATABASE_URL in a file, we can prefix all commands with symfony. This will detect services ran by Docker and/or SymfonyCloud (when the tunnel is open) and set the environment variable automatically.

Docker Compose and SymfonyCloud work seamlessly with Symfony thanks to these environment variables.

Check all exposed environment variables by executing symfony var:export:

```
$ symfony var:export
```

```
DATABASE_URL=postgres://main:main@127.0.0.1:32781/
main?sslmode=disable&charset=utf8
# ...
```

Remember the database *service name* used in the Docker and SymfonyCloud configurations? The service names are used as prefixes to define environment variables like DATABASE_URL. If your services are named according to the Symfony conventions, no other configuration is needed.

 Databases are not the only service that benefit from the Symfony conventions. The same goes for Mailer, for example (via the MAILER_DSN environment variable).

8.3 Changing the Default DATABASE_URL Value in .env

We will still change the .env file to setup the default DATABASE_DSN to use PostgreSQL:

```
--- a/.env
+++ b/.env
@@ -25,5 +25,5 @@ APP_SECRET=447c9fa8420eb53bbd4492194b87de8f
 # For an SQLite database, use: "sqlite:///%kernel.project_dir%/var/data.db"
 # For a PostgreSQL database, use:
"postgresql://db_user:db_password@127.0.0.1:5432/
db_name?serverVersion=11&charset=utf8"
 # IMPORTANT: You MUST configure your server version, either here or in config/
packages/doctrine.yaml
-DATABASE_URL=mysql://db_user:db_password@127.0.0.1:3306/
db_name?serverVersion=5.7
+DATABASE_URL=postgresql://127.0.0.1:5432/db?serverVersion=11&charset=utf8
 ###< doctrine/doctrine-bundle ###
```

Why does the information need to be duplicated in two different places? Because on some Cloud platforms, at *build time*, the database URL might not be known yet but Doctrine needs to know the database's engine to build its configuration. So, the host, username, and password do not really matter.

8.4 Creating Entity Classes

A conference can be described with a few properties:

- The *city* where the conference is organized;
- The *year* of the conference;
- An *international* flag to indicate if the conference is local or international (SymfonyLive vs SymfonyCon).

The Maker bundle can help us generate a class (an *Entity* class) that represents a conference:

```
$ symfony console make:entity Conference
```

This command is interactive: it will guide you through the process of adding all the fields you need. Use the following answers (most of them are the defaults, so you can hit the "Enter" key to use them):

- city, string, 255, no;
- year, string, 4, no;
- isInternational, boolean, no.

Here is the full output when running the command:

```
created: src/Entity/Conference.php
created: src/Repository/ConferenceRepository.php

Entity generated! Now let's add some fields!
You can always add more fields later manually or by re-running this command.

New property name (press <return> to stop adding fields):
> city

Field type (enter ? to see all types) [string]:
>

Field length [255]:
>

Can this field be null in the database (nullable) (yes/no) [no]:
>

updated: src/Entity/Conference.php

Add another property? Enter the property name (or press <return> to stop
adding fields):
> year

Field type (enter ? to see all types) [string]:
>

Field length [255]:
> 4

Can this field be null in the database (nullable) (yes/no) [no]:
>

updated: src/Entity/Conference.php

Add another property? Enter the property name (or press <return> to stop
adding fields):
> isInternational

Field type (enter ? to see all types) [boolean]:
>

Can this field be null in the database (nullable) (yes/no) [no]:
>

updated: src/Entity/Conference.php

Add another property? Enter the property name (or press <return> to stop
adding fields):
>


 Success!


Next: When you're ready, create a migration with make:migration
```

The Conference class has been stored under the App\Entity\ namespace.

The command also generated a Doctrine *repository* class: App\Repository\ConferenceRepository.

The generated code looks like the following (only a small portion of the file is replicated here):

src/App/Entity/Conference.php
```php
namespace App\Entity;

use App\Repository\ConferenceRepository;
use Doctrine\ORM\Mapping as ORM;

/**
 * @ORM\Entity(repositoryClass=ConferenceRepository::class)
 */
class Conference
{
    /**
     * @ORM\Id()
     * @ORM\GeneratedValue()
     * @ORM\Column(type="integer")
     */
    private $id;

    /**
     * @ORM\Column(type="string", length=255)
     */
    private $city;

    // ...

    public function getCity(): ?string
    {
        return $this->city;
    }

    public function setCity(string $city): self
    {
        $this->city = $city;

        return $this;
    }

    // ...
}
```

Note that the class itself is a plain PHP class with no signs of Doctrine. Annotations are used to add metadata useful for Doctrine to map the class to its related database table.

Doctrine added an id property to store the primary key of the row in the database table. This key (@ORM\Id()) is automatically generated (@ORM\GeneratedValue()) via a strategy that depends on the database engine.

Now, generate an Entity class for conference comments:

```
$ symfony console make:entity Comment
```

Enter the following answers:

- author, string, 255, no;
- text, text, no;
- email, string, 255, no;
- createdAt, datetime, no.

8.5 Linking Entities

The two entities, Conference and Comment, should be linked together. A Conference can have zero or more Comments, which is called a *one-to-many* relationship.

Use the make:entity command again to add this relationship to the Conference class:

```
$ symfony console make:entity Conference


 Your entity already exists! So let's add some new fields!

 New property name (press <return> to stop adding fields):
 > comments

 Field type (enter ? to see all types) [string]:
 > OneToMany

 What class should this entity be related to?:
 > Comment

 A new property will also be added to the Comment class...

 New field name inside Comment [conference]:
 >

 Is the Comment.conference property allowed to be null (nullable)? (yes/no)
 [yes]:
 > no

 Do you want to activate orphanRemoval on your relationship?
 A Comment is "orphaned" when it is removed from its related Conference.
 e.g. $conference->removeComment($comment)

 NOTE: If a Comment may *change* from one Conference to another, answer "no".
```

```
Do you want to automatically delete orphaned App\Entity\Comment objects
(orphanRemoval)? (yes/no) [no]:
> yes

updated: src/Entity/Conference.php
updated: src/Entity/Comment.php
```

 If you enter ? as an answer for the type, you will get all supported types:

```
Main types
  * string
  * text
  * boolean
  * integer (or smallint, bigint)
  * float

Relationships / Associations
  * relation (a wizard will help you build the relation)
  * ManyToOne
  * OneToMany
  * ManyToMany
  * OneToOne

Array/Object Types
  * array (or simple_array)
  * json
  * object
  * binary
  * blob

Date/Time Types
  * datetime (or datetime_immutable)
  * datetimetz (or datetimetz_immutable)
  * date (or date_immutable)
  * time (or time_immutable)
  * dateinterval

Other Types
  * decimal
  * guid
  * json_array
```

Have a look at the full diff for the entity classes after adding the relationship:

```
--- a/src/Entity/Comment.php
+++ b/src/Entity/Comment.php
@@ -36,6 +36,12 @@ class Comment
     */
    private $createdAt;
```

```
+    /**
+     * @ORM\ManyToOne(targetEntity=Conference::class, inversedBy="comments")
+     * @ORM\JoinColumn(nullable=false)
+     */
+    private $conference;
+
     public function getId(): ?int
     {
         return $this->id;
@@ -88,4 +94,16 @@ class Comment

         return $this;
     }
+
+    public function getConference(): ?Conference
+    {
+        return $this->conference;
+    }
+
+    public function setConference(?Conference $conference): self
+    {
+        $this->conference = $conference;
+
+        return $this;
+    }
 }
--- a/src/Entity/Conference.php
+++ b/src/Entity/Conference.php
@@ -2,6 +2,8 @@

 namespace App\Entity;

+use Doctrine\Common\Collections\ArrayCollection;
+use Doctrine\Common\Collections\Collection;
 use Doctrine\ORM\Mapping as ORM;

 /**
@@ -31,6 +33,16 @@ class Conference
     */
     private $isInternational;

+    /**
+     * @ORM\OneToMany(targetEntity=Comment::class, mappedBy="conference",
orphanRemoval=true)
+     */
+    private $comments;
+
+    public function __construct()
+    {
+        $this->comments = new ArrayCollection();
+    }
+
     public function getId(): ?int
     {
         return $this->id;
@@ -71,4 +83,35 @@ class Conference
```

```
        return $this;
    }

+
+   /**
+    * @return Collection|Comment[]
+    */
+   public function getComments(): Collection
+   {
+       return $this->comments;
+   }
+
+   public function addComment(Comment $comment): self
+   {
+       if (!$this->comments->contains($comment)) {
+           $this->comments[] = $comment;
+           $comment->setConference($this);
+       }
+
+       return $this;
+   }
+
+   public function removeComment(Comment $comment): self
+   {
+       if ($this->comments->contains($comment)) {
+           $this->comments->removeElement($comment);
+           // set the owning side to null (unless already changed)
+           if ($comment->getConference() === $this) {
+               $comment->setConference(null);
+           }
+       }
+
+       return $this;
+   }
}
```

Everything you need to manage the relationship has been generated for you. Once generated, the code becomes yours; feel free to customize it the way you want.

8.6 Adding more Properties

I just realized that we have forgotten to add one property on the Comment entity: attendees might want to attach a photo of the conference to illustrate their feedback.

Run make:entity once more and add a photoFilename property/column of type string, but allow it to be null as uploading a photo is optional:

```
$ symfony console make:entity Comment
```

8.7 Migrating the Database

The project model is now fully described by the two generated classes.

Next, we need to create the database tables related to these PHP entities.

Doctrine Migrations is the perfect match for such a task. It has already been installed as part of the `orm` dependency.

A *migration* is a class that describes the changes needed to update a database schema from its current state to the new one defined by the entity annotations. As the database is empty for now, the migration should consist of two table creations.

Let's see what Doctrine generates:

```
$ symfony console make:migration
```

Notice the generated file name in the output (a name that looks like `migrations/Version20191019083640.php`):

```
migrations/Version20191019083640.php
namespace DoctrineMigrations;

use Doctrine\DBAL\Schema\Schema;
use Doctrine\Migrations\AbstractMigration;

final class Version20191019083640 extends AbstractMigration
{
    public function up(Schema $schema) : void
    {
        // this up() migration is auto-generated, please modify it to your
needs
        $this->addSql('CREATE SEQUENCE comment_id_seq INCREMENT BY 1 MINVALUE
1 START 1');
        $this->addSql('CREATE SEQUENCE conference_id_seq INCREMENT BY 1
MINVALUE 1 START 1');
        $this->addSql('CREATE TABLE comment (id INT NOT NULL, conference_id
INT NOT NULL, author VARCHAR(255) NOT NULL, text TEXT NOT NULL, email
VARCHAR(255) NOT NULL, created_at TIMESTAMP(0) WITHOUT TIME ZONE NOT NULL,
photo_filename VARCHAR(255) DEFAULT NULL, PRIMARY KEY(id))');
        $this->addSql('CREATE INDEX IDX_9474526C604B8382 ON comment
(conference_id)');
        $this->addSql('CREATE TABLE conference (id INT NOT NULL, city
VARCHAR(255) NOT NULL, year VARCHAR(4) NOT NULL, is_international BOOLEAN NOT
NULL, PRIMARY KEY(id))');
        $this->addSql('ALTER TABLE comment ADD CONSTRAINT FK_9474526C604B8382
FOREIGN KEY (conference_id) REFERENCES conference (id) NOT DEFERRABLE
INITIALLY IMMEDIATE');
    }

    public function down(Schema $schema) : void
    {
```

```
        // ...
    }
}
```

8.8 Updating the Local Database

You can now run the generated migration to update the local database schema:

```
$ symfony console doctrine:migrations:migrate
```

The local database schema is now up-to-date, ready to store some data.

8.9 Updating the Production Database

The steps needed to migrate the production database are the same as the ones you are already familiar with: commit the changes and deploy.

When deploying the project, SymfonyCloud updates the code, but also runs the database migration if any (it detects if the `doctrine:migrations:migrate` command exists).

 Going Further

- *Databases and Doctrine ORM*[2] in Symfony applications;
- *SymfonyCasts Doctrine tutorial*[3];
- *Working with Doctrine Associations/Relations*[4];
- *DoctrineMigrationsBundle docs*[5].

2. https://symfony.com/doc/current/doctrine.html
3. https://symfonycasts.com/screencast/symfony-doctrine/install
4. https://symfony.com/doc/current/doctrine/associations.html
5. https://symfony.com/doc/master/bundles/DoctrineMigrationsBundle/index.html

Step 9

Setting up an Admin Backend

Adding upcoming conferences to the database is the job of project admins. An *admin backend* is a protected section of the website where *project admins* can manage the website data, moderate feedback submissions, and more.

How can we create this fast? By using a bundle that is able to generate an admin backend based on the project's model. EasyAdmin fits the bill perfectly.

9.1 Configuring EasyAdmin

First, add EasyAdmin as a project dependency:

```
$ symfony composer req "admin:^2.0"
```

To configure EasyAdmin, a new configuration file was generated via its Flex recipe:

config/packages/easy_admin.yaml

```
#easy_admin:
#    entities:
#        # List the entity class name you want to manage
#        - App\Entity\Product
#        - App\Entity\Category
#        - App\Entity\User
```

Almost all installed packages have a configuration like this one under the `config/packages/` directory. Most of the time, the defaults have been chosen carefully to work for most applications.

Uncomment the first couple of lines and add the project's model classes:

config/packages/easy_admin.yaml
```
easy_admin:
    entities:
        - App\Entity\Conference
        - App\Entity\Comment
```

Access the generated admin backend at `/admin`. Boom! A nice and feature-rich admin interface for conferences and comments:

 Why is the backend accessible under `/admin`? That's the default prefix configured in `config/routes/easy_admin.yaml`:

config/routes/easy_admin.yaml
```
easy_admin_bundle:
    resource: '@EasyAdminBundle/Controller/EasyAdminController.php'
    prefix: /admin
    type: annotation
```

You can change it to anything you like.

Adding conferences and comments is not possible yet as you would get an error: `Object of class App\Entity\Conference could not be converted to string`. EasyAdmin tries to display the conference related to comments, but it can only do so if there is a string representation of a conference. Fix it by adding a __toString() method on the Conference class:

```
--- a/src/Entity/Conference.php
+++ b/src/Entity/Conference.php
@@ -43,6 +43,11 @@ class Conference
         $this->comments = new ArrayCollection();
     }

+    public function __toString(): string
+    {
+        return $this->city.' '.$this->year;
+    }
+
     public function getId(): ?int
     {
         return $this->id;
```

Do the same for the Comment class:

```
--- a/src/Entity/Comment.php
+++ b/src/Entity/Comment.php
@@ -48,6 +48,11 @@ class Comment
     */
     private $photoFilename;

+    public function __toString(): string
+    {
+        return (string) $this->getEmail();
+    }
+
     public function getId(): ?int
     {
         return $this->id;
```

You can now add/modify/delete conferences directly from the admin backend. Play with it and add at least one conference.

Add some comments without photos. Set the date manually for now; we will fill-in the **createdAt** column automatically in a later step.

9.2 Customizing EasyAdmin

The default admin backend works well, but it can be customized in many ways to improve the experience. Let's do some simple changes to demonstrate the possibilities. Replace the current configuration with the following:

config/packages/easy_admin.yaml

```yaml
easy_admin:
    site_name: Conference Guestbook

    design:
        menu:
            - { route: 'homepage', label: 'Back to the website', icon: 'home' }
            - { entity: 'Conference', label: 'Conferences', icon: 'map-marker'
}
            - { entity: 'Comment', label: 'Comments', icon: 'comments' }

    entities:
        Conference:
            class: App\Entity\Conference

        Comment:
            class: App\Entity\Comment
            list:
                fields:
                    - author
                    - { property: 'email', type: 'email' }
                    - { property: 'createdAt', type: 'datetime' }
                sort: ['createdAt', 'ASC']
                filters: ['conference']
            edit:
                fields:
                    - { property: 'conference' }
                    - { property: 'createdAt', type: datetime, type_options: {
attr: { readonly: true } } }
                    - 'author'
                    - { property: 'email', type: 'email' }
                    - text
```

We have overridden the design section to add icons to the menu items
and to add a link back to the website home page.

For the Comment section, listing the fields lets us order them the way we
want. Some fields are tweaked, like setting the creation date to read-only.
The filters section defines which filters to expose on top of the regular
search field.

These customizations are just a small introduction of the possibilities given by EasyAdmin.

Play with the admin, filter the comments by conference, or search comments by email for instance. The only issue is that anybody can access the backend. Don't worry, we will secure it in a future step.

 Going Further

- *EasyAdmin docs*[1];
- *SymfonyCasts EasyAdminBundle tutorial*[2];
- *Symfony framework configuration reference*[3].

---

1. https://symfony.com/doc/master/bundles/EasyAdminBundle/index.html
2. https://symfonycasts.com/screencast/easyadminbundle
3. https://symfony.com/doc/current/reference/configuration/framework.html

Step 10

Building the User Interface

Everything is now in place to create the first version of the website user interface. We won't make it pretty. Just functional for now.

Remember the escaping we had to do in the controller for the easter egg to avoid security issues? We won't use PHP for our templates for that reason. Instead, we will use Twig. Besides handling output escaping for us, *Twig*[1] brings a lot of nice features we will leverage, like template inheritance.

10.1 Installing Twig

We don't need to add Twig as a dependency as it has already been installed as a *transitive dependency* of EasyAdmin. But what if you decide to switch to another admin bundle later on? One that uses an API and a React front-end for instance. It will probably not depend on Twig anymore, and so Twig will automatically be removed when you remove EasyAdmin.

For good measure, let's tell Composer that the project really depends on Twig, independently of EasyAdmin. Adding it like any other dependency is enough:

```
$ symfony composer req twig
```

---

1. https://twig.symfony.com/

Twig is now part of the main project dependencies in `composer.json`:

```
--- a/composer.json
+++ b/composer.json
@@ -14,6 +14,7 @@
        "symfony/framework-bundle": "4.4.*",
        "symfony/maker-bundle": "^1.0@dev",
        "symfony/orm-pack": "dev-master",
+       "symfony/twig-pack": "^1.0",
        "symfony/yaml": "4.4.*"
    },
    "require-dev": {
```

10.2 Using Twig for the Templates

All pages on the website will share the same *layout*. When installing Twig, a `templates/` directory has been created automatically and a sample layout was created as well in `base.html.twig`.

templates/base.html.twig
```
<!DOCTYPE html>
<html>
    <head>
        <meta charset="UTF-8">
        <title>{% block title %}Welcome!{% endblock %}</title>
        {% block stylesheets %}{% endblock %}
    </head>
    <body>
        {% block body %}{% endblock %}
        {% block javascripts %}{% endblock %}
    </body>
</html>
```

A layout can define `block` elements, which are the places where *child templates* that *extend* the layout add their contents.

Let's create a template for the project's homepage in `templates/conference/index.html.twig`:

templates/conference/index.html.twig
```
{% extends 'base.html.twig' %}

{% block title %}Conference Guestbook{% endblock %}

{% block body %}
    <h2>Give your feedback!</h2>

    {% for conference in conferences %}
        <h4>{{ conference }}</h4>
```

```
    {% endfor %}
{% endblock %}
```

The template *extends* `base.html.twig` and redefines the `title` and `body` blocks.

The `{% %}` notation in a template indicates *actions* and *structure*.

The `{{ }}` notation is used to *display* something. `{{ conference }}` displays the conference representation (the result of calling `__toString` on the `Conference` object).

10.3 Using Twig in a Controller

Update the controller to render the Twig template:

```
--- a/src/Controller/ConferenceController.php
+++ b/src/Controller/ConferenceController.php
@@ -2,24 +2,21 @@

 namespace App\Controller;

+use App\Repository\ConferenceRepository;
 use Symfony\Bundle\FrameworkBundle\Controller\AbstractController;
 use Symfony\Component\HttpFoundation\Response;
 use Symfony\Component\Routing\Annotation\Route;
+use Twig\Environment;

 class ConferenceController extends AbstractController
 {
     /**
      * @Route("/", name="homepage")
      */
-    public function index()
+    public function index(Environment $twig, ConferenceRepository
$conferenceRepository)
     {
-        return new Response(<<<EOF
-<html>
-    <body>
-        <img src="/images/under-construction.gif" />
-    </body>
-</html>
-EOF
-        );
+        return new Response($twig->render('conference/index.html.twig', [
+            'conferences' => $conferenceRepository->findAll(),
+        ]));
     }
 }
```

There is a lot going on here.

To be able to render a template, we need the Twig `Environment` object (the main Twig entry point). Notice that we ask for the Twig instance by type-hinting it in the controller method. Symfony is smart enough to know how to inject the right object.

We also need the conference repository to get all conferences from the database.

In the controller code, the `render()` method renders the template and passes an array of variables to the template. We are passing the list of `Conference` objects as a `conferences` variable.

A controller is a standard PHP class. We don't even need to extend the `AbstractController` class if we want to be explicit about our dependencies. You can remove it (but don't do it, as we will use the nice shortcuts it provides in future steps).

10.4 Creating the Page for a Conference

Each conference should have a dedicated page to list its comments. Adding a new page is a matter of adding a controller, defining a route for it, and creating the related template.

Add a `show()` method in `src/Controller/ConferenceController.php`:

```
--- a/src/Controller/ConferenceController.php
+++ b/src/Controller/ConferenceController.php
@@ -2,7 +2,9 @@

 namespace App\Controller;

+use App\Entity\Conference;
+use App\Repository\CommentRepository;
 use App\Repository\ConferenceRepository;
 use Symfony\Bundle\FrameworkBundle\Controller\AbstractController;
 use Symfony\Component\HttpFoundation\Response;
 use Symfony\Component\Routing\Annotation\Route;
@@ -19,4 +21,15 @@ class ConferenceController extends AbstractController
             'conferences' => $conferenceRepository->findAll(),
         ]));
     }
+
+    /**
+     * @Route("/conference/{id}", name="conference")
+     */
+    public function show(Environment $twig, Conference $conference,
CommentRepository $commentRepository)
+    {
+        return new Response($twig->render('conference/show.html.twig', [
+            'conference' => $conference,
+            'comments' => $commentRepository->findBy(['conference' =>
```

```
$conference], ['createdAt' => 'DESC']),
+        ]));
+    }
 }
```

This method has a special behavior we have not seen yet. We ask for a
`Conference` instance to be injected in the method. But there may be many
of these in the database. Symfony is able to determine which one you
want based on the `{id}` passed in the request path (`id` being the primary
key of the `conference` table in the database).

Retrieving the comments related to the conference can be done via the
`findBy()` method which takes a criteria as a first argument.

The last step is to create the `templates/conference/show.html.twig` file:

templates/conference/show.html.twig
```twig
{% extends 'base.html.twig' %}

{% block title %}Conference Guestbook - {{ conference }}{% endblock %}

{% block body %}
    <h2>{{ conference }} Conference</h2>

    {% if comments|length > 0 %}
        {% for comment in comments %}
            {% if comment.photofilename %}
                <img src="{{ asset('uploads/photos/' ~ comment.photofilename)
}}" />
            {% endif %}

            <h4>{{ comment.author }}</h4>
            <small>
                {{ comment.createdAt|format_datetime('medium', 'short') }}
            </small>

            <p>{{ comment.text }}</p>
        {% endfor %}
    {% else %}
        <div>No comments have been posted yet for this conference.</div>
    {% endif %}
{% endblock %}
```

In this template, we are using the | notation to call Twig *filters*. A filter
transforms a value. `comments|length` returns the number of comments
and `comment.createdAt|format_datetime('medium', 'short')` formats the
date in a human readable representation.

Try to reach the "first" conference via /conference/1, and notice the
following error:

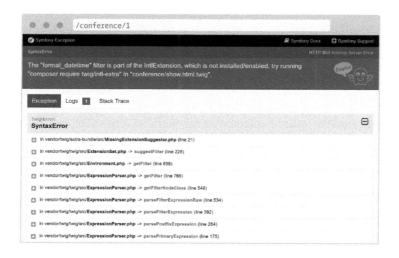

The error comes from the **format_datetime** filter as it is not part of Twig core. The error message gives you a hint about which package should be installed to fix the problem:

```
$ symfony composer require twig/intl-extra
```

Now the page works properly.

10.5 Linking Pages Together

The very last step to finish our first version of the user interface is to link the conference pages from the homepage:

```
--- a/templates/conference/index.html.twig
+++ b/templates/conference/index.html.twig
@@ -7,5 +7,8 @@
     {% for conference in conferences %}
        <h4>{{ conference }}</h4>
+       <p>
+           <a href="/conference/{{ conference.id }}">View</a>
+       </p>
     {% endfor %}
  {% endblock %}
```

But hard-coding a path is a bad idea for several reasons. The most important reason is if you change the path (from **/conference/{id}** to **/conferences/{id}** for instance), all links must be updated manually.

Instead, use the **path()** Twig *function* and use the *route name*:

```
--- a/templates/conference/index.html.twig
+++ b/templates/conference/index.html.twig
@@ -8,7 +8,7 @@
    {% for conference in conferences %}
        <h4>{{ conference }}</h4>
        <p>
-            <a href="/conference/{{ conference.id }}">View</a>
+            <a href="{{ path('conference', { id: conference.id }) }}">View</a>
        </p>
    {% endfor %}
 {% endblock %}
```

The `path()` function generates the path to a page using its route name.
The values of the route parameters are passed as a Twig map.

10.6 Paginating the Comments

With thousands of attendees, we can expect quite a few comments. If we
display them all on a single page, it will grow very fast.

Create a `getCommentPaginator()` method in the Comment Repository that
returns a Comment *Paginator* based on a conference and an offset (where
to start):

```
--- a/src/Repository/CommentRepository.php
+++ b/src/Repository/CommentRepository.php
@@ -3,8 +3,10 @@
 namespace App\Repository;

 use App\Entity\Comment;
+use App\Entity\Conference;
 use Doctrine\Bundle\DoctrineBundle\Repository\ServiceEntityRepository;
 use Doctrine\Persistence\ManagerRegistry;
+use Doctrine\ORM\Tools\Pagination\Paginator;

 /**
  * @method Comment|null find($id, $lockMode = null, $lockVersion = null)
@@ -14,11 +16,27 @@ use Doctrine\Persistence\ManagerRegistry;
  */
 class CommentRepository extends ServiceEntityRepository
 {
+    public const PAGINATOR_PER_PAGE = 2;
+
     public function __construct(ManagerRegistry $registry)
     {
         parent::__construct($registry, Comment::class);
     }

+    public function getCommentPaginator(Conference $conference, int $offset):
Paginator
+    {
```

```
+           $query = $this->createQueryBuilder('c')
+               ->andWhere('c.conference = :conference')
+               ->setParameter('conference', $conference)
+               ->orderBy('c.createdAt', 'DESC')
+               ->setMaxResults(self::PAGINATOR_PER_PAGE)
+               ->setFirstResult($offset)
+               ->getQuery()
+           ;
+
+           return new Paginator($query);
+       }
+
        // /**
        // * @return Comment[] Returns an array of Comment objects
        // */
```

We have set the maximum number of comments per page to 2 to ease
testing.

To manage the pagination in the template, pass the Doctrine Paginator
instead of the Doctrine Collection to Twig:

```
--- a/src/Controller/ConferenceController.php
+++ b/src/Controller/ConferenceController.php
@@ -6,6 +6,7 @@ use App\Entity\Conference;
 use App\Repository\CommentRepository;
 use App\Repository\ConferenceRepository;
 use Symfony\Bundle\FrameworkBundle\Controller\AbstractController;
+use Symfony\Component\HttpFoundation\Request;
 use Symfony\Component\HttpFoundation\Response;
 use Symfony\Component\Routing\Annotation\Route;
 use Twig\Environment;
@@ -25,11 +26,16 @@ class ConferenceController extends AbstractController
     /**
      * @Route("/conference/{id}", name="conference")
      */
-    public function show(Environment $twig, Conference $conference,
CommentRepository $commentRepository)
+    public function show(Request $request, Environment $twig, Conference
$conference, CommentRepository $commentRepository)
     {
+        $offset = max(0, $request->query->getInt('offset', 0));
+        $paginator = $commentRepository->getCommentPaginator($conference,
$offset);
+
         return new Response($twig->render('conference/show.html.twig', [
             'conference' => $conference,
-            'comments' => $commentRepository->findBy(['conference' =>
$conference], ['createdAt' => 'DESC']),
+            'comments' => $paginator,
+            'previous' => $offset - CommentRepository::PAGINATOR_PER_PAGE,
+            'next' => min(count($paginator), $offset +
CommentRepository::PAGINATOR_PER_PAGE),
         ]));
     }
```

```
    }
```

The controller gets the offset from the Request query string ($request->query) as an integer (getInt()), defaulting to 0 if not available.

The previous and next offsets are computed based on all the information we have from the paginator.

Finally, update the template to add links to the next and previous pages:

```
index 0c9e7d2..14b51fd 100644
--- a/templates/conference/show.html.twig
+++ b/templates/conference/show.html.twig
@@ -6,6 +6,8 @@
    <h2>{{ conference }} Conference</h2>

    {% if comments|length > 0 %}
+        <div>There are {{ comments|length }} comments.</div>
+
        {% for comment in comments %}
            {% if comment.photofilename %}
                <img src="{{ asset('uploads/photos/' ~ comment.photofilename)
}}" />
@@ -18,6 +20,13 @@
                <p>{{ comment.text }}</p>
        {% endfor %}
+
+        {% if previous >= 0 %}
+            <a href="{{ path('conference', { id: conference.id, offset:
previous }) }}">Previous</a>
+        {% endif %}
+        {% if next < comments|length %}
+            <a href="{{ path('conference', { id: conference.id, offset: next
}) }}">Next</a>
+        {% endif %}
    {% else %}
        <div>No comments have been posted yet for this conference.</div>
    {% endif %}
```

You should now be able to navigate the comments via the "Previous" and "Next" links:

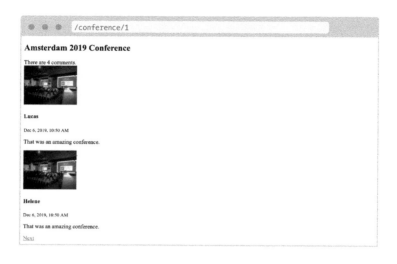

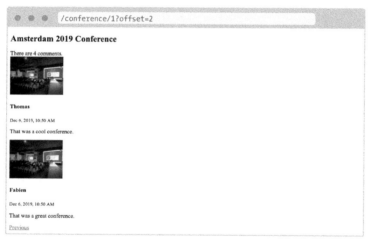

10.7 Refactoring the Controller

You might have noticed that both methods in `ConferenceController` take a Twig environment as an argument. Instead of injecting it into each method, let's use some constructor injection instead (that makes the list of arguments shorter and less redundant):

```
--- a/src/Controller/ConferenceController.php
+++ b/src/Controller/ConferenceController.php
@@ -13,12 +13,19 @@ use Twig\Environment;

 class ConferenceController extends AbstractController
 {
```

```
+    private $twig;
+
+    public function __construct(Environment $twig)
+    {
+        $this->twig = $twig;
+    }
+
    /**
     * @Route("/", name="homepage")
     */
-    public function index(Environment $twig, ConferenceRepository
$conferenceRepository)
+    public function index(ConferenceRepository $conferenceRepository)
    {
-        return new Response($twig->render('conference/index.html.twig', [
+        return new Response($this->twig->render('conference/index.html.twig',
[
            'conferences' => $conferenceRepository->findAll(),
        ]));
    }
@@ -26,12 +33,12 @@ class ConferenceController extends AbstractController
    /**
     * @Route("/conference/{id}", name="conference")
     */
-    public function show(Request $request, Environment $twig, Conference
$conference, CommentRepository $commentRepository)
+    public function show(Request $request, Conference $conference,
CommentRepository $commentRepository)
    {
        $offset = max(0, $request->query->getInt('offset', 0));
        $paginator = $commentRepository->getCommentPaginator($conference,
$offset);

-        return new Response($twig->render('conference/show.html.twig', [
+        return new Response($this->twig->render('conference/show.html.twig', [
            'conference' => $conference,
            'comments' => $paginator,
            'previous' => $offset - CommentRepository::PAGINATOR_PER_PAGE,
```

 Going Further

- *Twig docs*[2];
- *Creating and Using Templates*[3] in Symfony applications;
- *SymfonyCasts Twig tutorial*[4];
- *Twig functions and filters only available in Symfony*[5];
- The *AbstractController base controller*[6].

---

2. https://twig.symfony.com/doc/2.x/
3. https://symfony.com/doc/current/templates.html

93

4. https://symfonycasts.com/screencast/symfony/twig-recipe
5. https://symfony.com/doc/current/reference/twig_reference.html
6. https://symfony.com/doc/current/controller.html#the-base-controller-classes-services

Step 11
Branching the Code

There are many ways to organize the workflow of code changes in a project. But working directly on the Git master branch and deploying directly to production without testing is probably not the best one.

Testing is not just about unit or functional tests, it is also about checking the application behavior with production data. If you or your *stakeholders*[1] can browse the application exactly as it will be deployed to end users, this becomes a huge advantage and allows you to deploy with confidence. It is especially powerful when non-technical people can validate new features.

We will continue doing all the work in the Git master branch in the next steps for simplicity sake and to avoid repeating ourselves, but let's see how this could work better.

11.1 Adopting a Git Workflow

One possible workflow is to create one branch per new feature or bug fix. It is simple and efficient.

---

1. https://en.wikipedia.org/wiki/Project_stakeholder

11.2 Describing your Infrastructure

You might not have realized it yet, but having the infrastructure stored in files alongside of the code helps a lot. Docker and SymfonyCloud use configuration files to describe the project infrastructure. When a new feature needs an additional service, the code changes and the infrastructure changes are part of the same patch.

11.3 Creating Branches

The workflow starts with the creation of a Git branch:

```
$ git checkout -b sessions-in-redis
```

This command creates a `sessions-in-redis` branch from the `master` branch. It "forks" the code and the infrastructure configuration.

11.4 Storing Sessions in Redis

As you might have guessed from the branch name, we want to switch session storage from the filesystem to a Redis store.

The needed steps to make it a reality are typical:

1. Create a Git branch;
2. Update the Symfony configuration if needed;
3. Write and/or update some code if needed;
4. Update the PHP configuration (add the Redis PHP extension);
5. Update the infrastructure on Docker and SymfonyCloud (add the Redis service);
6. Test locally;
7. Test remotely;
8. Merge the branch to master;
9. Deploy to production;
10. Delete the branch.

All changes needed for 2 to 5 can be done in one patch:

```
--- a/.symfony.cloud.yaml
+++ b/.symfony.cloud.yaml
@@ -15,8 +15,13 @@ runtime:
 build:
     flavor: none

+variables:
+    php-ext:
+        redis: 5.3.1
+
 relationships:
     database: "db:postgresql"
+    redis: "rediscache:redis"

 web:
     locations:
--- a/.symfony/services.yaml
+++ b/.symfony/services.yaml
@@ -2,3 +2,6 @@ db:
     type: postgresql:11
     disk: 1024
     size: S
+
+rediscache:
+    type: redis:5.0
--- a/config/packages/framework.yaml
+++ b/config/packages/framework.yaml
@@ -7,7 +7,7 @@ framework:
     # Enables session support. Note that the session will ONLY be started if
you read or write from it.
     # Remove or comment this section to explicitly disable session support.
     session:
-        handler_id: null
+        handler_id: '%env(REDIS_URL)%'
         cookie_secure: auto
         cookie_samesite: lax

--- a/docker-compose.yaml
+++ b/docker-compose.yaml
@@ -8,3 +8,7 @@ services:
             POSTGRES_PASSWORD: main
             POSTGRES_DB: main
         ports: [5432]
+
+    redis:
+        image: redis:5-alpine
+        ports: [6379]
```

Isn't it *beautiful*?

"Reboot" Docker to start the Redis service:

```
$ docker-compose stop
$ docker-compose up -d
```

I'll let you test locally by browsing the website. As there are no visual changes and because we are not using sessions yet, everything should still work as before.

11.5 Deploying a Branch

Before deploying to production, we should test the branch on the same infrastructure as the production one. We should also validate that everything works fine for the Symfony `prod` environment (the local website used the Symfony `dev` environment).

First, make sure to commit your changes to the new branch:

```
$ git add .
$ git commit -m'Configure redis sessions'
```

Now, let's create a *SymfonyCloud environment* based on the *Git branch*:

```
$ symfony env:create
```

This command creates a new environment as follows:

- The branch inherits the code and infrastructure from the current Git branch (`sessions-in-redis`);
- The data come from the master (aka production) environment by taking a consistent snapshot of all service data, including files (user uploaded files for instance) and databases;
- A new dedicated cluster is created to deploy the code, the data, and the infrastructure.

As the deployment follows the same steps as deploying to production, database migrations will also be executed. This is a great way to validate that the migrations work with production data.

The non-`master` environments are very similar to the `master` one except for some small differences: for instance, emails are not sent by default.

Once the deployment is finished, open the new branch in a browser:

```
$ symfony open:remote
```

Note that all SymfonyCloud commands work on the current Git branch. This command opens the deployed URL for the `sessions-in-redis` branch; the URL will look like `https://sessions-in-redis-xxx.eu.s5y.io/`.

Test the website on this new environment, you should see all the data that you created in the master environment.

If you add more conferences on the `master` environment, they won't show up in the `sessions-in-redis` environment and vice-versa. The environments are independent and isolated.

If the code evolves on master, you can always rebase the Git branch and deploy the updated version, resolving the conflicts for both the code and the infrastructure.

You can even synchronize the data from master back to the `sessions-in-redis` environment:

```
$ symfony env:sync
```

11.6 Debugging Production Deployments before Deploying

By default, all SymfonyCloud environments use the same settings as the `master/prod` environment (aka the Symfony `prod` environment). This allows you to test the application in real-life conditions. It gives you the feeling of developing and testing directly on production servers, but without the risks associated with it. This reminds me of the good old days when we were deploying via FTP.

In case of a problem, you might want to switch to the `dev` Symfony environment:

```
$ symfony env:debug
```

When done, move back to production settings:

```
$ symfony env:debug --off
```

 Never enable the `dev` environment and never enable the Symfony Profiler on the `master` branch; it would make your application really slow and open a lot of serious security vulnerabilities.

11.7 Testing Production Deployments before Deploying

Having access to the upcoming version of the website with production data opens up a lot of opportunities: from visual regression testing to performance testing. *Blackfire*[2] is the perfect tool for the job.

Refer to the step about "Performance" to learn more about how you can use Blackfire to test your code before deploying.

11.8 Merging to Production

When you are satisfied with the branch changes, merge the code and the infrastructure back to the Git master branch:

```
$ git checkout master
$ git merge sessions-in-redis
```

And deploy:

```
$ symfony deploy
```

When deploying, only the code and infrastructure changes are pushed to SymfonyCloud; the data are not affected in any way.

11.9 Cleaning up

Finally, clean up by removing the Git branch and the SymfonyCloud environment:

```
$ git branch -d sessions-in-redis
$ symfony env:delete --env=sessions-in-redis --no-interaction
```

 Going Further

- *Git branching*[3];
- *Redis docs*[4].

---

2. https://blackfire.io

3. https://www.git-scm.com/book/en/v2/Git-Branching-Branches-in-a-Nutshell
4. https://redis.io/documentation

Step 12
Listening to Events

The current layout is missing a navigation header to go back to the homepage or switch from one conference to the next.

12.1 Adding a Website Header

Anything that should be displayed on all web pages, like a header, should be part of the main base layout:

```
--- a/templates/base.html.twig
+++ b/templates/base.html.twig
@@ -6,6 +6,15 @@
        {% block stylesheets %}{% endblock %}
    </head>
    <body>
+        <header>
+            <h1><a href="{{ path('homepage') }}">Guestbook</a></h1>
+            <ul>
+            {% for conference in conferences %}
+                <li><a href="{{ path('conference', { id: conference.id })
}}">{{ conference }}</a></li>
+            {% endfor %}
+            </ul>
+            <hr />
+        </header>
        {% block body %}{% endblock %}
        {% block javascripts %}{% endblock %}
    </body>
```

Adding this code to the layout means that all templates extending it must

define a `conferences` variable, which must be created and passed from
their controllers.

As we only have two controllers, you might do the following:

```
--- a/src/Controller/ConferenceController.php
+++ b/src/Controller/ConferenceController.php
@@ -32,9 +32,10 @@ class ConferenceController extends AbstractController
     /**
      * @Route("/conference/{slug}", name="conference")
      */
-    public function show(Conference $conference, CommentRepository
$commentRepository)
+    public function show(Conference $conference, CommentRepository
$commentRepository, ConferenceRepository $conferenceRepository)
     {
         return new Response($this->twig->render('conference/show.html.twig', [
+            'conferences' => $conferenceRepository->findAll(),
             'conference' => $conference,
             'comments' => $commentRepository->findBy(['conference' =>
$conference], ['createdAt' => 'DESC']),
         ]));
```

Imagine having to update dozens of controllers. And doing the same on
all new ones. This is not very practical. There must be a better way.

Twig has the notion of global variables. A *global variable* is available in
all rendered templates. You can define them in a configuration file, but
it only works for static values. To add all conferences as a Twig global
variable, we are going to create a listener.

12.2 Discovering Symfony Events

Symfony comes built-in with an Event Dispatcher Component. A
dispatcher *dispatches* certain *events* at specific times that *listeners* can
listen to. Listeners are hooks into the framework internals.

For instance, some events allow you to interact with the lifecycle of
HTTP requests. During the handling of a request, the dispatcher
dispatches events when a request has been created, when a controller is
about to be executed, when a response is ready to be sent, or when an
exception has been thrown. A *listener* can listen to one or more events
and execute some logic based on the event context.

Events are well-defined extension points that make the framework more
generic and extensible. Many Symfony Components like Security,
Messenger, Workflow, or Mailer use them extensively.

Another built-in example of events and listeners in action is the lifecycle
of a command: you can create a listener to execute code before *any*

command is run.

Any package or bundle can also dispatch their own events to make their code extensible.

To avoid having a configuration file that describes which events a listener wants to listen to, create a *subscriber*. A subscriber is a listener with a static getSubscribedEvents() method that returns its configuration. This allows subscribers to be registered in the Symfony dispatcher automatically.

12.3 Implementing a Subscriber

You know the song by heart now, use the maker bundle to generate a subscriber:

```
$ symfony console make:subscriber TwigEventSubscriber
```

The command asks you about which event you want to listen to. Choose the Symfony\Component\HttpKernel\Event\ControllerEvent event, which is dispatched just before the controller is called. It is the best time to inject the conferences global variable so that Twig will have access to it when the controller will render the template. Update your subscriber as follows:

```
--- a/src/EventSubscriber/TwigEventSubscriber.php
+++ b/src/EventSubscriber/TwigEventSubscriber.php
@@ -2,14 +2,25 @@

 namespace App\EventSubscriber;

+use App\Repository\ConferenceRepository;
 use Symfony\Component\EventDispatcher\EventSubscriberInterface;
 use Symfony\Component\HttpKernel\Event\ControllerEvent;
+use Twig\Environment;

 class TwigEventSubscriber implements EventSubscriberInterface
 {
+    private $twig;
+    private $conferenceRepository;
+
+    public function __construct(Environment $twig, ConferenceRepository
$conferenceRepository)
+    {
+        $this->twig = $twig;
+        $this->conferenceRepository = $conferenceRepository;
+    }
+
     public function onControllerEvent(ControllerEvent $event)
```

```
    {
-       // ...
+       $this->twig->addGlobal('conferences', $this->conferenceRepository-
>findAll());
    }

    public static function getSubscribedEvents()
```

Now, you can add as many controllers as you want: the `conferences`
variable will always be available in Twig.

 We will talk about a much better alternative performance-wise in
a later step.

12.4 Sorting Conferences by Year and City

Ordering the conference list by year may facilitate browsing. We could
create a custom method to retrieve and sort all conferences, but instead,
we are going to override the default implementation of the `findAll()`
method to be sure that sorting applies everywhere:

```
--- a/src/Repository/ConferenceRepository.php
+++ b/src/Repository/ConferenceRepository.php
@@ -19,6 +19,11 @@ class ConferenceRepository extends ServiceEntityRepository
        parent::__construct($registry, Conference::class);
    }

+   public function findAll()
+   {
+       return $this->findBy([], ['year' => 'ASC', 'city' => 'ASC']);
+   }
+
    // /**
    //  * @return Conference[] Returns an array of Conference objects
    //  */
```

At the end of this step, the website should look like the following:

106

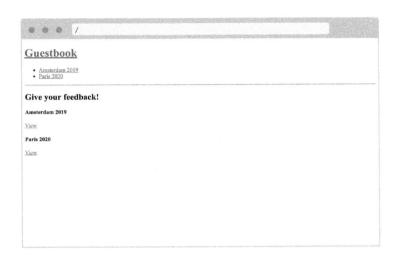

Going Further

- The *Request-Response Flow*[1] in Symfony applications;
- The *built-in Symfony HTTP events*[2];
- The *built-in Symfony Console events*[3].

---

1. https://symfony.com/doc/current/components/http_kernel.html#the-workflow-of-a-request
2. https://symfony.com/doc/current/reference/events.html
3. https://symfony.com/doc/current/components/console/events.html

Step 13

Managing the Lifecycle of Doctrine Objects

When creating a new comment, it would be great if the `createdAt` date would be set automatically to the current date and time.

Doctrine has different ways to manipulate objects and their properties during their lifecycle (before the row in the database is created, after the row is updated, ...).

13.1 Defining Lifecycle Callbacks

When the behavior does not need any service and should be applied to only one kind of entity, define a callback in the entity class:

```
--- a/src/Entity/Comment.php
+++ b/src/Entity/Comment.php
@@ -7,6 +7,7 @@ use Doctrine\ORM\Mapping as ORM;

 /**
  * @ORM\Entity(repositoryClass=CommentRepository::class)
+ * @ORM\HasLifecycleCallbacks()
  */
 class Comment
 {
@@ -106,6 +107,14 @@ class Comment
         return $this;
```

```
        }
+       /**
+        * @ORM\PrePersist
+        */
+       public function setCreatedAtValue()
+       {
+           $this->createdAt = new \DateTime();
+       }
+
        public function getConference(): ?Conference
        {
            return $this->conference;
```

The `@ORM\PrePersist` *event* is triggered when the object is stored in the database for the very first time. When that happens, the `setCreatedAtValue()` method is called and the current date and time is used for the value of the `createdAt` property.

13.2 Adding Slugs to Conferences

The URLs for conferences are not meaningful: `/conference/1`. More importantly, they depend on an implementation detail (the primary key in the database is leaked).

What about using URLs like `/conference/paris-2020` instead? That would look much better. `paris-2020` is what we call the conference *slug*.

Add a new `slug` property for conferences (a not nullable string of 255 characters):

```
$ symfony console make:entity Conference
```

Create a migration file to add the new column:

```
$ symfony console make:migration
```

And execute that new migration:

```
$ symfony console doctrine:migrations:migrate
```

Got an error? This is expected. Why? Because we asked for the slug to be not `null` but existing entries in the conference database will get a `null` value when the migration is ran. Let's fix that by tweaking the migration:

```
--- a/migrations/Version00000000000000.php
```

```
+++ b/migrations/Version00000000000000.php
@@ -20,7 +20,9 @@ final class Version20200714152808 extends AbstractMigration
    public function up(Schema $schema) : void
    {
        // this up() migration is auto-generated, please modify it to your
needs
-       $this->addSql('ALTER TABLE conference ADD slug VARCHAR(255) NOT
NULL');
+       $this->addSql('ALTER TABLE conference ADD slug VARCHAR(255)');
+       $this->addSql("UPDATE conference SET slug=CONCAT(LOWER(city), '-',
year)");
+       $this->addSql('ALTER TABLE conference ALTER COLUMN slug SET NOT
NULL');
    }

    public function down(Schema $schema) : void
```

The trick here is to add the column and allow it to be null, then set the slug to a not null value, and finally, change the slug column to not allow null.

 For a real project, using CONCAT(LOWER(city), '-', year) might not be enough. In that case, we would need to use the "real" Slugger.

Migration should run fine now:

```
$ symfony console doctrine:migrations:migrate
```

Because the application will soon use slugs to find each conference, let's tweak the Conference entity to ensure that slug values are unique in the database:

```
--- a/src/Entity/Conference.php
+++ b/src/Entity/Conference.php
@@ -5,9 +5,11 @@ namespace App\Entity;
 use Doctrine\Common\Collections\ArrayCollection;
 use Doctrine\Common\Collections\Collection;
 use Doctrine\ORM\Mapping as ORM;
+use Symfony\Bridge\Doctrine\Validator\Constraints\UniqueEntity;

 /**
  * @ORM\Entity(repositoryClass=ConferenceRepository::class)
+ * @UniqueEntity("slug")
  */
 class Conference
 {
@@ -39,7 +41,7 @@ class Conference
     private $comments;

     /**
```

```
-     * @ORM\Column(type="string", length=255)
+     * @ORM\Column(type="string", length=255, unique=true)
     */
    private $slug;
```

As you might have guessed, we need to perform the migration dance:

```
$ symfony console make:migration
```

```
$ symfony console doctrine:migrations:migrate
```

13.3 Generating Slugs

Generating a slug that reads well in a URL (where anything besides ASCII characters should be encoded) is a challenging task, especially for languages other than English. How do you convert é to e for instance?

Instead of reinventing the wheel, let's use the Symfony `String` component, which eases the manipulation of strings and provides a *slugger*:

```
$ symfony composer req string
```

Add a `computeSlug()` method to the `Conference` class that computes the slug based on the conference data:

```
--- a/src/Entity/Conference.php
+++ b/src/Entity/Conference.php
@@ -6,6 +6,7 @@ use Doctrine\Common\Collections\ArrayCollection;
 use Doctrine\Common\Collections\Collection;
 use Doctrine\ORM\Mapping as ORM;
 use Symfony\Bridge\Doctrine\Validator\Constraints\UniqueEntity;
+use Symfony\Component\String\Slugger\SluggerInterface;

 /**
  * @ORM\Entity(repositoryClass=ConferenceRepository::class)
@@ -60,6 +61,13 @@ class Conference
         return $this->id;
     }

+    public function computeSlug(SluggerInterface $slugger)
+    {
+        if (!$this->slug || '-' === $this->slug) {
+            $this->slug = (string) $slugger->slug((string) $this)->lower();
+        }
+    }
+
```

```php
public function getCity(): ?string
{
    return $this->city;
```

The computeSlug() method only computes a slug when the current slug is
empty or set to the special - value. Why do we need the - special value?
Because when adding a conference in the backend, the slug is required.
So, we need a non-empty value that tells the application that we want the
slug to be automatically generated.

13.4 Defining a Complex Lifecycle Callback

As for the createdAt property, the slug one should be set automatically
whenever the conference is updated by calling the computeSlug() method.

But as this method depends on a SluggerInterface implementation, we
cannot add a prePersist event as before (we don't have a way to inject
the slugger).

Instead, create a Doctrine entity listener:

src/EntityListener/ConferenceEntityListener.php
```php
namespace App\EntityListener;

use App\Entity\Conference;
use Doctrine\ORM\Event\LifecycleEventArgs;
use Symfony\Component\String\Slugger\SluggerInterface;

class ConferenceEntityListener
{
    private $slugger;

    public function __construct(SluggerInterface $slugger)
    {
        $this->slugger = $slugger;
    }

    public function prePersist(Conference $conference, LifecycleEventArgs $event)
    {
        $conference->computeSlug($this->slugger);
    }

    public function preUpdate(Conference $conference, LifecycleEventArgs $event)
    {
        $conference->computeSlug($this->slugger);
    }
}
```

Note that the slug is updated when a new conference is created (`prePersist()`) and whenever it is updated (`preUpdate()`).

13.5 Configuring a Service in the Container

Up until now, we have not talked about one key component of Symfony, the *dependency injection container*. The container is responsible for managing *services*: creating them and injecting them whenever needed.

A *service* is a "global" object that provides features (e.g. a mailer, a logger, a slugger, etc.) unlike *data objects* (e.g. Doctrine entity instances).

You rarely interact with the container directly as it automatically injects service objects whenever you need them: the container injects the controller argument objects when you type-hint them for instance.

If you wondered how the event listener was registered in the previous step, you now have the answer: the container. When a class implements some specific interfaces, the container knows that the class needs to be registered in a certain way.

Unfortunately, automation is not provided for everything, especially for third-party packages. The entity listener that we just wrote is one such example; it cannot be managed by the Symfony service container automatically as it does not implement any interface and it does not extend a "well-know class".

We need to partially declare the listener in the container. The dependency wiring can be omitted as it can still be guessed by the container, but we need to manually add some *tags* to register the listener with the Doctrine event dispatcher:

```
--- a/config/services.yaml
+++ b/config/services.yaml
@@ -25,3 +25,7 @@ services:

     # add more service definitions when explicit configuration is needed
     # please note that last definitions always *replace* previous ones
+    App\EntityListener\ConferenceEntityListener:
+        tags:
+            - { name: 'doctrine.orm.entity_listener', event: 'prePersist',
entity: 'App\Entity\Conference'}
+            - { name: 'doctrine.orm.entity_listener', event: 'preUpdate',
entity: 'App\Entity\Conference'}
```

Don't confuse Doctrine event listeners and Symfony ones. Even if they look very similar, they are not using the same infrastructure under the hood.

13.6 Using Slugs in the Application

Try adding more conferences in the backend and change the city or the year of an existing one; the slug won't be updated except if you use the special - value.

The last change is to update the controllers and the templates to use the conference slug instead of the conference id for routes:

```
--- a/src/Controller/ConferenceController.php
+++ b/src/Controller/ConferenceController.php
@@ -31,7 +31,7 @@ class ConferenceController extends AbstractController
     }

     /**
-     * @Route("/conference/{id}", name="conference")
+     * @Route("/conference/{slug}", name="conference")
     */
    public function show(Request $request, Conference $conference,
CommentRepository $commentRepository)
    {
--- a/templates/base.html.twig
+++ b/templates/base.html.twig
@@ -10,7 +10,7 @@
            <h1><a href="{{ path('homepage') }}">Guestbook</a></h1>
            <ul>
            {% for conference in conferences %}
-                <li><a href="{{ path('conference', { id: conference.id })
}}">{{ conference }}</a></li>
+                <li><a href="{{ path('conference', { slug: conference.slug })
}}">{{ conference }}</a></li>
            {% endfor %}
            </ul>
            <hr />
--- a/templates/conference/show.html.twig
+++ b/templates/conference/show.html.twig
@@ -22,10 +22,10 @@
        {% endfor %}

        {% if previous >= 0 %}
-            <a href="{{ path('conference', { id: conference.id, offset:
previous }) }}">Previous</a>
+            <a href="{{ path('conference', { slug: conference.slug, offset:
previous }) }}">Previous</a>
        {% endif %}
        {% if next < comments|length %}
-            <a href="{{ path('conference', { id: conference.id, offset: next
```

```
}) }}">Next</a>
+              <a href="{{ path('conference', { slug: conference.slug, offset:
next }) }}">Next</a>
         {% endif %}
    {% else %}
         <div>No comments have been posted yet for this conference.</div>
--- a/templates/conference/index.html.twig
+++ b/templates/conference/index.html.twig
@@ -8,7 +8,7 @@
    {% for conference in conferences %}
         <h4>{{ conference }}</h4>
         <p>
-             <a href="{{ path('conference', { id: conference.id }) }}">View</a>
+             <a href="{{ path('conference', { slug: conference.slug })
}}">View</a>
         </p>
    {% endfor %}
 {% endblock %}
```

Accessing conference pages should now be done via its slug:

Going Further

- The *Doctrine event system*[1] (lifecycle callbacks and listeners, entity listeners and lifecycle subscribers);

- The *String component docs*[2];

- The *Service container*[3];

- The *Symfony Services Cheat Sheet*[4].

1. https://symfony.com/doc/current/doctrine/events.html
2. https://symfony.com/doc/master/components/string.html
3. https://symfony.com/doc/current/service_container.html
4. https://github.com/andreia/symfony-cheat-sheets/blob/master/Symfony4/services_en_42.pdf

Step 14
Accepting Feedback with Forms

Time to let our attendees give feedback on conferences. They will contribute their comments through an *HTML form*.

14.1 Generating a Form Type

Use the Maker bundle to generate a form class:

```
$ symfony console make:form CommentFormType Comment
```

```
created: src/Form/CommentFormType.php
```

```
Success!
```

```
Next: Add fields to your form and start using it.
Find the documentation at https://symfony.com/doc/current/forms.html
```

The `App\Form\CommentFormType` class defines a form for the `App\Entity\Comment` entity:

src/App/Form/CommentFormType.php
```
namespace App\Form;

use App\Entity\Comment;
use Symfony\Component\Form\AbstractType;
```

```
use Symfony\Component\Form\FormBuilderInterface;
use Symfony\Component\OptionsResolver\OptionsResolver;

class CommentFormType extends AbstractType
{
    public function buildForm(FormBuilderInterface $builder, array $options)
    {
        $builder
            ->add('author')
            ->add('text')
            ->add('email')
            ->add('createdAt')
            ->add('photoFilename')
            ->add('conference')
        ;
    }

    public function configureOptions(OptionsResolver $resolver)
    {
        $resolver->setDefaults([
            'data_class' => Comment::class,
        ]);
    }
}
```

A *form type*[1] describes the *form fields* bound to a model. It does the
data conversion between submitted data and the model class properties.
By default, Symfony uses metadata from the Comment entity - such as
the Doctrine metadata - to guess configuration about each field. For
example, the text field renders as a textarea because it uses a larger
column in the database.

14.2 Displaying a Form

To display the form to the user, create the form in the controller and pass
it to the template:

```
--- a/src/Controller/ConferenceController.php
+++ b/src/Controller/ConferenceController.php
@@ -2,7 +2,9 @@

 namespace App\Controller;

+use App\Entity\Comment;
 use App\Entity\Conference;
+use App\Form\CommentFormType;
 use App\Repository\CommentRepository;
 use App\Repository\ConferenceRepository;
```

---

1. https://symfony.com/doc/current/forms.html#form-types

```
use Symfony\Bundle\FrameworkBundle\Controller\AbstractController;
@@ -35,6 +37,9 @@ class ConferenceController extends AbstractController
     */
    public function show(Request $request, Conference $conference,
CommentRepository $commentRepository)
    {
+       $comment = new Comment();
+       $form = $this->createForm(CommentFormType::class, $comment);
+
        $offset = max(0, $request->query->getInt('offset', 0));
        $paginator = $commentRepository->getCommentPaginator($conference,
$offset);

@@ -43,6 +48,7 @@ class ConferenceController extends AbstractController
            'comments' => $paginator,
            'previous' => $offset - CommentRepository::PAGINATOR_PER_PAGE,
            'next' => min(count($paginator), $offset +
CommentRepository::PAGINATOR_PER_PAGE),
+           'comment_form' => $form->createView(),
        ]));
    }
 }
```

You should never instantiate the form type directly. Instead, use the
`createForm()` method. This method is part of `AbstractController` and
eases the creation of forms.

When passing a form to a template, use `createView()` to convert the data
to a format suitable for templates.

Displaying the form in the template can be done via the `form` Twig
function:

```
--- a/templates/conference/show.html.twig
+++ b/templates/conference/show.html.twig
@@ -21,4 +21,8 @@
    {% else %}
        <div>No comments have been posted yet for this conference.</div>
    {% endif %}
+
+   <h2>Add your own feedback</h2>
+
+   {{ form(comment_form) }}
 {% endblock %}
```

When refreshing a conference page in the browser, note that each form
field shows the right HTML widget (the data type is derived from the
model):

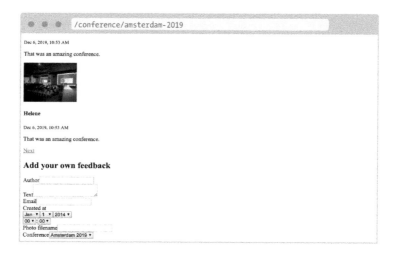

The form() function generates the HTML form based on all the information defined in the Form type. It also adds enctype=multipart/form-data on the <form> tag as required by the file upload input field. Moreover, it takes care of displaying error messages when the submission has some errors. Everything can be customized by overriding the default templates, but we won't need it for this project.

14.3 Customizing a Form Type

Even if form fields are configured based on their model counterpart, you can customize the default configuration in the form type class directly:

```
--- a/src/Form/CommentFormType.php
+++ b/src/Form/CommentFormType.php
@@ -4,20 +4,31 @@ namespace App\Form;

 use App\Entity\Comment;
 use Symfony\Component\Form\AbstractType;
+use Symfony\Component\Form\Extension\Core\Type\EmailType;
+use Symfony\Component\Form\Extension\Core\Type\FileType;
+use Symfony\Component\Form\Extension\Core\Type\SubmitType;
 use Symfony\Component\Form\FormBuilderInterface;
 use Symfony\Component\OptionsResolver\OptionsResolver;
+use Symfony\Component\Validator\Constraints\Image;

 class CommentFormType extends AbstractType
 {
     public function buildForm(FormBuilderInterface $builder, array $options)
     {
         $builder
-            ->add('author')
```

```
+            ->add('author', null, [
+                'label' => 'Your name',
+            ])
         ->add('text')
-            ->add('email')
-            ->add('createdAt')
-            ->add('photoFilename')
-            ->add('conference')
+            ->add('email', EmailType::class)
+            ->add('photo', FileType::class, [
+                'required' => false,
+                'mapped' => false,
+                'constraints' => [
+                    new Image(['maxSize' => '1024k'])
+                ],
+            ])
+            ->add('submit', SubmitType::class)
        ;
    }
```

Note that we have added a submit button (that allows us to keep using the simple `{{ form(comment_form) }}` expression in the template).

Some fields cannot be auto-configured, like the `photoFilename` one. The `Comment` entity only needs to save the photo filename, but the form has to deal with the file upload itself. To handle this case, we have added a field called `photo` as un-`mapped` field: it won't be mapped to any property on `Comment`. We will manage it manually to implement some specific logic (like storing the uploaded photo on the disk).

As an example of customization, we have also modified the default label for some fields.

123

14.4 Validating Models

The Form Type configures the frontend rendering of the form (via some HTML5 validation). Here is the generated HTML form:

```html
<form name="comment_form" method="post" enctype="multipart/form-data">
    <div id="comment_form">
        <div >
            <label for="comment_form_author" class="required">Your name</label>
            <input type="text" id="comment_form_author"
name="comment_form[author]" required="required" maxlength="255" />
        </div>
        <div >
            <label for="comment_form_text" class="required">Text</label>
            <textarea id="comment_form_text" name="comment_form[text]"
required="required"></textarea>
        </div>
        <div >
            <label for="comment_form_email" class="required">Email</label>
            <input type="email" id="comment_form_email"
name="comment_form[email]" required="required" />
        </div>
        <div >
            <label for="comment_form_photo">Photo</label>
            <input type="file" id="comment_form_photo"
name="comment_form[photo]" />
        </div>
        <div >
            <button type="submit" id="comment_form_submit"
name="comment_form[submit]">Submit</button>
        </div>
        <input type="hidden" id="comment_form__token"
name="comment_form[_token]"
value="DwqsEanxc48jofxsqbGBVLQBqlVJ_Tg4u9-BL1Hjgac" />
    </div>
</form>
```

The form uses the `email` input for the comment email and makes most of the fields `required`. Note that the form also contains a `_token` hidden field to protect the form from *CSRF attacks*[2].

But if the form submission bypasses the HTML validation (by using an HTTP client that does not enforce these validation rules like cURL), invalid data can hit the server.

We also need to add some validation constraints on the `Comment` data model:

```
--- a/src/Entity/Comment.php
+++ b/src/Entity/Comment.php
@@ -3,6 +3,7 @@
```

---

2. https://owasp.org/www-community/attacks/csrf

```
 namespace App\Entity;

 use App\Repository\CommentRepository;
 use Doctrine\ORM\Mapping as ORM;
+use Symfony\Component\Validator\Constraints as Assert;

 /**
  * @ORM\Entity(repositoryClass=CommentRepository::class)
@@ -19,16 +20,20 @@ class Comment

     /**
      * @ORM\Column(type="string", length=255)
+     * @Assert\NotBlank
      */
     private $author;

     /**
      * @ORM\Column(type="text")
+     * @Assert\NotBlank
      */
     private $text;

     /**
      * @ORM\Column(type="string", length=255)
+     * @Assert\NotBlank
+     * @Assert\Email
      */
     private $email;
```

14.5 Handling a Form

The code we have written so far is enough to display the form.

We should now handle the form submission and the persistence of its information to the database in the controller:

```
--- a/src/Controller/ConferenceController.php
+++ b/src/Controller/ConferenceController.php
@@ -7,6 +7,7 @@ use App\Entity\Conference;
 use App\Form\CommentFormType;
 use App\Repository\CommentRepository;
 use App\Repository\ConferenceRepository;
+use Doctrine\ORM\EntityManagerInterface;
 use Symfony\Bundle\FrameworkBundle\Controller\AbstractController;
 use Symfony\Component\HttpFoundation\Request;
 use Symfony\Component\HttpFoundation\Response;
@@ -16,10 +17,12 @@ use Twig\Environment;
 class ConferenceController extends AbstractController
 {
     private $twig;
+    private $entityManager;
```

```
-    public function __construct(Environment $twig)
+    public function __construct(Environment $twig, EntityManagerInterface
$entityManager)
     {
         $this->twig = $twig;
+        $this->entityManager = $entityManager;
     }

     /**
@@ -39,6 +42,15 @@ class ConferenceController extends AbstractController
     {
         $comment = new Comment();
         $form = $this->createForm(CommentFormType::class, $comment);
+        $form->handleRequest($request);
+        if ($form->isSubmitted() && $form->isValid()) {
+            $comment->setConference($conference);
+
+            $this->entityManager->persist($comment);
+            $this->entityManager->flush();
+
+            return $this->redirectToRoute('conference', ['slug' =>
$conference->getSlug()]);
+        }

         $offset = max(0, $request->query->getInt('offset', 0));
         $paginator = $commentRepository->getCommentPaginator($conference,
$offset);
```

When the form is submitted, the Comment object is updated according to the submitted data.

The conference is forced to be the same as the one from the URL (we removed it from the form).

If the form is not valid, we display the page, but the form will now contain submitted values and error messages so that they can be displayed back to the user.

Try the form. It should work well and the data should be stored in the database (check it in the admin backend). There is one problem though: photos. They do not work as we have not handled them yet in the controller.

14.6 Uploading Files

Uploaded photos should be stored on the local disk, somewhere accessible by the frontend so that we can display them on the conference page. We will store them under the public/uploads/photos directory:

```
--- a/src/Controller/ConferenceController.php
```

```
+++ b/src/Controller/ConferenceController.php
@@ -10,6 +10,7 @@ use App\Repository\ConferenceRepository;
 use Doctrine\ORM\EntityManagerInterface;
 use Doctrine\ORM\Tools\Pagination\Paginator;
 use Symfony\Bundle\FrameworkBundle\Controller\AbstractController;
+use Symfony\Component\HttpFoundation\File\Exception\FileException;
 use Symfony\Component\HttpFoundation\Request;
 use Symfony\Component\HttpFoundation\Response;
 use Symfony\Component\Routing\Annotation\Route;
@@ -37,7 +38,7 @@ class ConferenceController extends AbstractController
     /**
      * @Route("/conference/{slug}", name="conference")
      */
-    public function show(Request $request, Conference $conference,
CommentRepository $commentRepository)
+    public function show(Request $request, Conference $conference,
CommentRepository $commentRepository, string $photoDir)
     {
         $comment = new Comment();
         $form = $this->createForm(CommentFormType::class, $comment);
@@ -45,6 +46,15 @@ class ConferenceController extends AbstractController
         $form->handleRequest($request);
         if ($form->isSubmitted() && $form->isValid()) {
             $comment->setConference($conference);
+            if ($photo = $form['photo']->getData()) {
+                $filename = bin2hex(random_bytes(6)).'.'.$photo-
>guessExtension();
+                try {
+                    $photo->move($photoDir, $filename);
+                } catch (FileException $e) {
+                    // unable to upload the photo, give up
+                }
+                $comment->setPhotoFilename($filename);
+            }

             $this->entityManager->persist($comment);
             $this->entityManager->flush();
```

To manage photo uploads, we create a random name for the file. Then,
we move the uploaded file to its final location (the photo directory).
Finally, we store the filename in the Comment object.

Notice the new argument on the show() method? $photoDir is a string and
not a service. How can Symfony know what to inject here? The Symfony
Container is able to store *parameters* in addition to services. Parameters
are scalars that help configure services. These parameters can be injected
into services explicitly, or they can be *bound by name*:

```
--- a/config/services.yaml
+++ b/config/services.yaml
@@ -10,6 +10,8 @@ services:
   _defaults:
     autowire: true        # Automatically injects dependencies in your
```

```
services.
        autoconfigure: true # Automatically registers your services as
commands, event subscribers, etc.
+       bind:
+               $photoDir: "%kernel.project_dir%/public/uploads/photos"

    # makes classes in src/ available to be used as services
    # this creates a service per class whose id is the fully-qualified class
name
```

The bind setting allows Symfony to inject the value whenever a service
has a $photoDir argument.

Try to upload a PDF file instead of a photo. You should see the error
messages in action. The design is quite ugly at the moment, but don't
worry, everything will turn beautiful in a few steps when we will work
on the design of the website. For the forms, we will change one line of
configuration to style all form elements.

14.7 Debugging Forms

When a form is submitted and something does not work quite well, use
the "Form" panel of the Symfony Profiler. It gives you information about
the form, all its options, the submitted data and how they are converted
internally. If the form contains any errors, they will be listed as well.

The typical form workflow goes like this:

- The form is displayed on a page;
- The user submits the form via a POST request;
- The server redirects the user to another page or the same page.

But how can you access the profiler for a successful submit request?
Because the page is immediately redirected, we never see the web debug
toolbar for the POST request. No problem: on the redirected page, hover
over the left "200" green part. You should see the "302" redirection with
a link to the profile (in parenthesis).

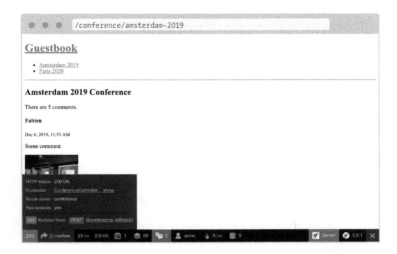

Click on it to access the POST request profile, and go to the "Form" panel:

14.8 Displaying Uploaded Photos in the Admin Backend

The admin backend is currently displaying the photo filename, but we want to see the actual photo:

```
--- a/config/packages/easy_admin.yaml
+++ b/config/packages/easy_admin.yaml
@@ -8,6 +8,7 @@ easy_admin:
            fields:
                - author
                - { property: 'email', type: 'email' }
+                - { property: 'photoFilename', type: 'image',
'base_path': "/uploads/photos", label: 'Photo' }
                - { property: 'createdAt', type: 'datetime' }
        edit:
            fields:
```

14.9 Excluding Uploaded Photos from Git

Don't commit yet! We don't want to store uploaded images in the Git repository. Add the /public/uploads directory to the .gitignore file:

```
--- a/.gitignore
+++ b/.gitignore
@@ -1,3 +1,4 @@
+/public/uploads

 ###> symfony/framework-bundle ###
 /.env.local
```

14.10 Storing Uploaded Files on Production Servers

The last step is to store the uploaded files on production servers. Why would we have to do something special? Because most modern cloud platforms use read-only containers for various reasons. SymfonyCloud is no exception.

Not everything is read-only in a Symfony project. We try hard to generate as much cache as possible when building the container (during the cache warmup phase), but Symfony still needs to be able to write somewhere for the user cache, the logs, the sessions if they are stored on the filesystem, and more.

Have a look at `.symfony.cloud.yaml`, there is already a writeable *mount* for the `var/` directory. The `var/` directory is the only directory where Symfony writes (caches, logs, ...).

Let's create a new mount for uploaded photos:

```
--- a/.symfony.cloud.yaml
+++ b/.symfony.cloud.yaml
@@ -26,6 +26,7 @@ disk: 512

 mounts:
     "/var": { source: local, source_path: var }
+    "/public/uploads": { source: local, source_path: uploads }

 hooks:
     build: |
```

You can now deploy the code and photos will be stored in the `public/uploads/` directory like our local version.

 Going Further

- *SymfonyCasts Forms tutorial*[3];
- How to *customize Symfony Form rendering in HTML*[4];
- *Validating Symfony Forms*[5];
- The *Symfony Form Types reference*[6];
- The *FlysystemBundle docs*[7], which provides integration with multiple cloud storage providers, such as AWS S3, Azure and Google Cloud Storage;
- The *Symfony Configuration Parameters*[8].
- The *Symfony Validation Constraints*[9];
- The *Symfony Form Cheat Sheet*[10].

3. https://symfonycasts.com/screencast/symfony-forms
4. https://symfony.com/doc/current/form/form_customization.html
5. https://symfony.com/doc/current/forms.html#validating-forms
6. https://symfony.com/doc/current/reference/forms/types.html
7. https://github.com/thephpleague/flysystem-bundle/blob/master/docs/1-getting-started.md
8. https://symfony.com/doc/current/configuration.html#configuration-parameters
9. https://symfony.com/doc/current/validation.html#basic-constraints
10. https://github.com/andreia/symfony-cheat-sheets/blob/master/Symfony2/how_symfony2_forms_works_en.pdf

Step 15
Securing the Admin Backend

The admin backend interface should only be accessible by trusted people. Securing this area of the website can be done using the Symfony Security component.

Like for Twig, the security component is already installed via transitive dependencies. Let's add it explicitly to the project's `composer.json` file:

```
$ symfony composer req security
```

15.1 Defining a User Entity

Even if attendees won't be able to create their own accounts on the website, we are going to create a fully functional authentication system for the admin. We will therefore only have one user, the website admin.

The first step is to define a `User` entity. To avoid any confusions, let's name it `Admin` instead.

To integrate the `Admin` entity with the Symfony Security authentication system, it needs to follow some specific requirements. For instance, it needs a `password` property.

Use the dedicated `make:user` command to create the `Admin` entity instead of the traditional `make:entity` one:

```
$ symfony console make:user Admin
```

Answer the interactive questions: we want to use Doctrine to store the admins (**yes**), use `username` for the unique display name of admins, and each user will have a password (**yes**).

The generated class contains methods like `getRoles()`, `eraseCredentials()`, and a few others that are needed by the Symfony authentication system.

If you want to add more properties to the `Admin` user, use `make:entity`.

Let's add a `__toString()` method as EasyAdmin likes those:

```
--- a/src/Entity/Admin.php
+++ b/src/Entity/Admin.php
@@ -74,6 +74,11 @@ class Admin implements UserInterface
         return $this;
     }

+    public function __toString(): string
+    {
+        return $this->username;
+    }
+
    /**
     * @see UserInterface
     */
```

In addition to generating the `Admin` entity, the command also updated the security configuration to wire the entity with the authentication system:

```
--- a/config/packages/security.yaml
+++ b/config/packages/security.yaml
@@ -1,7 +1,15 @@
 security:
+    encoders:
+        App\Entity\Admin:
+            algorithm: auto
+
     # https://symfony.com/doc/current/security.html#where-do-users-come-from-
user-providers
     providers:
-        in_memory: { memory: null }
+        # used to reload user from session & other features (e.g. switch_user)
+        app_user_provider:
+            entity:
+                class: App\Entity\Admin
+                property: username
     firewalls:
         dev:
             pattern: ^/(_(profiler|wdt)|css|images|js)/
```

We let Symfony select the best possible algorithm for encoding passwords (which will evolve over time).

Time to generate a migration and migrate the database:

```
$ symfony console make:migration
$ symfony console doctrine:migrations:migrate -n
```

15.2 Generating a Password for the Admin User

We won't develop a dedicated system to create admin accounts. Again, we will only ever have one admin. The login will be `admin` and we need to encode the password.

Choose whatever you like as a password and run the following command to generate the encoded password:

```
$ symfony console security:encode-password


Symfony Password Encoder Utility
================================

 Type in your password to be encoded:
 >

 ------------------
 --------------------------------------------------------------------------------
  Key                 Value
 ------------------
 --------------------------------------------------------------------------------
  Encoder used        Symfony\Component\Security\Core\Encoder\MigratingPasswordEncoder
  Encoded password
$argon2id$v=19$m=65536,t=4,p=1$BQG+jovPcunctc3OxG5PxQ$TiGbx451NKdo+g9vLtfkMy4KjASKSOcnNxjij4gT
 ------------------
 --------------------------------------------------------------------------------

 ! [NOTE] Self-salting encoder used: the encoder generated its own built-in salt.


[OK] Password encoding succeeded
```

15.3 Creating an Admin

Insert the admin user via an SQL statement:

```
$ symfony run psql -c "INSERT INTO admin (id, username, roles, password) \
  VALUES (nextval('admin_id_seq'), 'admin', '[\"ROLE_ADMIN\"]', \

 '\$argon2id\$v=19\$m=65536,t=4,p=1\$BQG+jovPcunctc3OxG5PxQ\$TiGbx451NKdo+g9vLtfkMy4KjASKSOcnNx
```

Note the escaping of the $ sign in the password column value; escape them all!

15.4 Configuring the Security Authentication

Now that we have an admin user, we can secure the admin backend. Symfony supports several authentication strategies. Let's use a classic and popular *form authentication system*.

Run the `make:auth` command to update the security configuration, generate a login template, and create an *authenticator*:

```
$ symfony console make:auth
```

Select 1 to generate a login form authenticator, name the authenticator class `AppAuthenticator`, the controller `SecurityController`, and generate a `/logout` URL (yes).

The command updated the security configuration to wire the generated classes:

```
--- a/config/packages/security.yaml
+++ b/config/packages/security.yaml
@@ -16,6 +16,13 @@ security:
            security: false
        main:
            anonymous: lazy
+            guard:
+                authenticators:
+                    - App\Security\AppAuthenticator
+            logout:
+                path: app_logout
+                # where to redirect after logout
+                # target: app_any_route

            # activate different ways to authenticate
            # https://symfony.com/doc/current/security.html#firewalls-
authentication
```

As hinted by the command output, we need to customize the route in the `onAuthenticationSuccess()` method to redirect the user when they successfully sign in:

```
--- a/src/Security/AppAuthenticator.php
+++ b/src/Security/AppAuthenticator.php
@@ -94,8 +94,7 @@ class AppAuthenticator extends
AbstractFormLoginAuthenticator implements Passwor
            return new RedirectResponse($targetPath);
        }

-        // For example : return new RedirectResponse($this->urlGenerator-
```

136

```
>generate('some_route'));
-        throw new \Exception('TODO: provide a valid redirect inside
'.__FILE__);
+        return new RedirectResponse($this->urlGenerator-
>generate('easyadmin'));
    }

    protected function getLoginUrl()
```

 How do I know that the EasyAdmin route is **easyadmin**? I don't.
But I ran the following command that shows the association
between route names and paths:

```
$ symfony console debug:router
```

15.5 Adding Authorization Access Control Rules

A security system is made of two parts: *authentication* and *authorization*.
When creating the admin user, we gave them the ROLE_ADMIN role. Let's
restrict the /admin section to users having this role by adding a rule to
access_control:

```
--- a/config/packages/security.yaml
+++ b/config/packages/security.yaml
@@ -33,5 +33,5 @@ security:
    # Easy way to control access for large sections of your site
    # Note: Only the *first* access control that matches will be used
    access_control:
-        # - { path: ^/admin, roles: ROLE ADMIN }
+        - { path: ^/admin, roles: ROLE_ADMIN }
        # - { path: ^/profile, roles: ROLE_USER }
```

The access_control rules restrict access by regular expressions. When
trying to access a URL that starts with /admin, the security system will
check for the ROLE_ADMIN role on the logged-in user.

15.6 Authenticating via the Login Form

If you try to access the admin backend, you should now be redirected to
the login page and prompted to enter a login and a password:

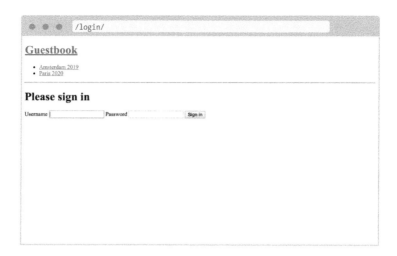

Log in using `admin` and whatever plain-text password you encoded earlier. If you copied my SQL command exactly, the password is `admin`.

Note that EasyAdmin automatically recognizes the Symfony authentication system:

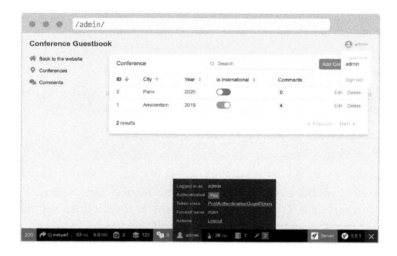

Try to click on the "Sign out" link. You have it! A fully-secured backend admin.

 If you want to create a fully-featured form authentication system, have a look at the `make:registration-form` command.

Going Further

- The *Symfony Security docs*[1];
- *SymfonyCasts Security tutorial*[2];
- *How to Build a Login Form*[3] in Symfony applications;
- The *Symfony Security Cheat Sheet*[4].

---

1. https://symfony.com/doc/current/security.html
2. https://symfonycasts.com/screencast/symfony-security
3. https://symfony.com/doc/current/security/form_login_setup.html
4. https://github.com/andreia/symfony-cheat-sheets/blob/master/Symfony4/security_en_44.pdf

Step 16

Preventing Spam with an API

Anyone can submit a feedback. Even robots, spammers, and more. We could add some "captcha" to the form to somehow be protected from robots, or we can use some third-party APIs.

I have decided to use the free *Akismet*[1] service to demonstrate how to call an API and how to make the call "out of band".

16.1 Signing up on Akismet

Sign-up for a free account on *akismet.com*[2] and get the Akismet API key.

16.2 Depending on Symfony HTTPClient Component

Instead of using a library that abstracts the Akismet API, we will do all the API calls directly. Doing the HTTP calls ourselves is more efficient (and allows us to benefit from all the Symfony debugging tools like the integration with the Symfony Profiler).

To make API calls, use the Symfony HttpClient Component:

```
$ symfony composer req http-client
```

---

1. https://akismet.com
2. https://akismet.com

16.3 Designing a Spam Checker Class

Create a new class under `src/` named `SpamChecker` to wrap the logic of calling the Akismet API and interpreting its responses:

src/SpamChecker.php

```php
namespace App;

use App\Entity\Comment;
use Symfony\Contracts\HttpClient\HttpClientInterface;

class SpamChecker
{
    private $client;
    private $endpoint;

    public function __construct(HttpClientInterface $client, string $akismetKey)
    {
        $this->client = $client;
        $this->endpoint = sprintf('https://%s.rest.akismet.com/1.1/comment-check', $akismetKey);
    }

    /**
     * @return int Spam score: 0: not spam, 1: maybe spam, 2: blatant spam
     *
     * @throws \RuntimeException if the call did not work
     */
    public function getSpamScore(Comment $comment, array $context): int
    {
        $response = $this->client->request('POST', $this->endpoint, [
            'body' => array_merge($context, [
                'blog' => 'https://guestbook.example.com',
                'comment_type' => 'comment',
                'comment_author' => $comment->getAuthor(),
                'comment_author_email' => $comment->getEmail(),
                'comment_content' => $comment->getText(),
                'comment_date_gmt' => $comment->getCreatedAt()->format('c'),
                'blog_lang' => 'en',
                'blog_charset' => 'UTF-8',
                'is_test' => true,
            ]),
        ]);

        $headers = $response->getHeaders();
        if ('discard' === ($headers['x-akismet-pro-tip'][0] ?? '')) {
            return 2;
        }

        $content = $response->getContent();
        if (isset($headers['x-akismet-debug-help'][0])) {
            throw new \RuntimeException(sprintf('Unable to check for spam: %s (%s).', $content, $headers['x-akismet-debug-help'][0]));
        }
```

```
        return 'true' === $content ? 1 : 0;
    }
}
```

The HTTP client request() method submits a POST request to the Akismet URL ($this->endpoint) and passes an array of parameters.

The getSpamScore() method returns 3 values depending on the API call response:

- 2: if the comment is a "blatant spam";
- 1: if the comment might be spam;
- 0: if the comment is not spam (ham).

 Use the special akismet-guaranteed-spam@example.com email address to force the result of the call to be spam.

16.4 Using Environment Variables

The SpamChecker class relies on an $akismetKey argument. Like for the upload directory, we can inject it via a bind container setting:

```
--- a/config/services.yaml
+++ b/config/services.yaml
@@ -12,6 +12,7 @@ services:
        autoconfigure: true # Automatically registers your services as
commands, event subscribers, etc.
        bind:
            $photoDir: "%kernel.project_dir%/public/uploads/photos"
+           $akismetKey: "%env(AKISMET_KEY)%"

    # makes classes in src/ available to be used as services
    # this creates a service per class whose id is the fully-qualified class
name
```

We certainly don't want to hard-code the value of the Akismet key in the services.yaml configuration file, so we are using an environment variable instead (AKISMET_KEY).

It is then up to each developer to set a "real" environment variable or to store the value in a .env.local file:

.env.local

```
AKISMET_KEY=abcdef
```

For production, a "real" environment variable should be defined.

That works well, but managing many environment variables might become cumbersome. In such a case, Symfony has a "better" alternative when it comes to storing secrets.

16.5 Storing Secrets

Instead of using many environment variables, Symfony can manage a *vault* where you can store many secrets. One key feature is the ability to commit the vault in the repository (but without the key to open it). Another great feature is that it can manage one vault per environment.

Secrets are environment variables in disguise.

Add the Akismet key in the vault:

```
$ symfony console secrets:set AKISMET_KEY


 Please type the secret value:
 >

 [OK] Secret "AKISMET_KEY" encrypted in "config/secrets/dev/"; you can commit
it.
```

Because this is the first time we have run this command, it generated two keys into the `config/secret/dev/` directory. It then stored the `AKISMET_KEY` secret in that same directory.

For development secrets, you can decide to commit the vault and the keys that have been generated in the `config/secret/dev/` directory.

Secrets can also be overridden by setting an environment variable of the same name.

16.6 Checking Comments for Spam

One simple way to check for spam when a new comment is submitted is to call the spam checker before storing the data into the database:

```
--- a/src/Controller/ConferenceController.php
+++ b/src/Controller/ConferenceController.php
```

```
@@ -7,6 +7,7 @@ use App\Entity\Conference;
 use App\Form\CommentFormType;
 use App\Repository\CommentRepository;
 use App\Repository\ConferenceRepository;
+use App\SpamChecker;
 use Doctrine\ORM\EntityManagerInterface;
 use Symfony\Bundle\FrameworkBundle\Controller\AbstractController;
 use Symfony\Component\HttpFoundation\File\Exception\FileException;
@@ -39,7 +40,7 @@ class ConferenceController extends AbstractController
     /**
      * @Route("/conference/{slug}", name="conference")
      */
-    public function show(Request $request, Conference $conference,
CommentRepository $commentRepository, string $photoDir)
+    public function show(Request $request, Conference $conference,
CommentRepository $commentRepository, SpamChecker $spamChecker, string
$photoDir)
     {
         $comment = new Comment();
         $form = $this->createForm(CommentFormType::class, $comment);
@@ -58,6 +59,17 @@ class ConferenceController extends AbstractController
         }

         $this->entityManager->persist($comment);
+
+        $context = [
+            'user_ip' => $request->getClientIp(),
+            'user_agent' => $request->headers->get('user-agent'),
+            'referrer' => $request->headers->get('referer'),
+            'permalink' => $request->getUri(),
+        ];
+        if (2 === $spamChecker->getSpamScore($comment, $context)) {
+            throw new \RuntimeException('Blatant spam, go away!');
+        }
+
         $this->entityManager->flush();

         return $this->redirectToRoute('conference', ['slug' =>
$conference->getSlug()]);
```

Check that it works fine.

16.7 Managing Secrets in Production

For production, SymfonyCloud supports setting *sensitive environment variables*:

```
$ symfony var:set --sensitive AKISMET_KEY=abcdef
```

But as discussed above, using Symfony secrets might be better. Not in terms of security, but in terms of secret management for the project's team. All secrets are stored in the repository and the only environment variable you need to manage for production is the decryption key. That makes it possible for anyone in the team to add production secrets even if they don't have access to production servers. The setup is a bit more involved though.

First, generate a pair of keys for production use:

```
$ APP_ENV=prod symfony console secrets:generate-keys
```

Re-add the Akismet secret in the production vault but with its production value:

```
$ APP_ENV=prod symfony console secrets:set AKISMET_KEY
```

The last step is to send the decryption key to SymfonyCloud by setting a sensitive variable:

```
$ symfony var:set --sensitive SYMFONY_DECRYPTION_SECRET=`php -r 'echo base64_encode(include("config/secrets/prod/prod.decrypt.private.php"));'`
```

You can add and commit all files; the decryption key has been added in .gitignore automatically, so it will never be committed. For more safety, you can remove it from your local machine as it has been deployed now:

```
$ rm -f config/secrets/prod/prod.decrypt.private.php
```

 ## Going Further

- The *HttpClient component docs*[3];
- The *Environment Variable Processors*[4];
- The *Symfony HttpClient Cheat Sheet*[5].

---

3. https://symfony.com/doc/current/components/http_client.html
4. https://symfony.com/doc/current/configuration/env_var_processors.html
5. https://github.com/andreia/symfony-cheat-sheets/blob/master/Symfony4/httpclient_en_43.pdf

Step 17

Testing

As we start to add more and more functionality to the application, it is probably the right time to talk about testing.

Fun fact: I found a bug while writing the tests in this chapter.

Symfony relies on PHPUnit for unit tests. Let's install it:

```
$ symfony composer req phpunit
```

17.1 Writing Unit Tests

SpamChecker is the first class we are going to write tests for. Generate a unit test:

```
$ symfony console make:unit-test SpamCheckerTest
```

Testing the SpamChecker is a challenge as we certainly don't want to hit the Akismet API. We are going to *mock* the API.

Let's write a first test for when the API returns an error:

```
--- a/tests/SpamCheckerTest.php
+++ b/tests/SpamCheckerTest.php
@@ -2,12 +2,26 @@

 namespace App\Tests;
```

```
+use App\Entity\Comment;
+use App\SpamChecker;
 use PHPUnit\Framework\TestCase;
+use Symfony\Component\HttpClient\MockHttpClient;
+use Symfony\Component\HttpClient\Response\MockResponse;
+use Symfony\Contracts\HttpClient\ResponseInterface;

 class SpamCheckerTest extends TestCase
 {
-    public function testSomething()
+    public function testSpamScoreWithInvalidRequest()
     {
-        $this->assertTrue(true);
+        $comment = new Comment();
+        $comment->setCreatedAtValue();
+        $context = [];
+
+        $client = new MockHttpClient([new MockResponse('invalid',
['response_headers' => ['x-akismet-debug-help: Invalid key']])]);
+        $checker = new SpamChecker($client, 'abcde');
+
+        $this->expectException(\RuntimeException::class);
+        $this->expectExceptionMessage('Unable to check for spam: invalid
(Invalid key).');
+        $checker->getSpamScore($comment, $context);
     }
 }
```

The `MockHttpClient` class makes it possible to mock any HTTP server. It takes an array of `MockResponse` instances that contain the expected body and Response headers.

Then, we call the `getSpamScore()` method and check that an exception is thrown via the `expectException()` method of PHPUnit.

Run the tests to check that they pass:

```
$ symfony php bin/phpunit
```

Let's add tests for the happy path:

```
--- a/tests/SpamCheckerTest.php
+++ b/tests/SpamCheckerTest.php
@@ -24,4 +24,32 @@ class SpamCheckerTest extends TestCase
         $this->expectExceptionMessage('Unable to check for spam: invalid
(Invalid key).');
         $checker->getSpamScore($comment, $context);
     }
+
+    /**
+     * @dataProvider getComments
+     */
+    public function testSpamScore(int $expectedScore, ResponseInterface
```

```
 $response, Comment $comment, array $context)
+    {
+        $client = new MockHttpClient([$response]);
+        $checker = new SpamChecker($client, 'abcde');
+
+        $score = $checker->getSpamScore($comment, $context);
+        $this->assertSame($expectedScore, $score);
+    }
+
+    public function getComments(): iterable
+    {
+        $comment = new Comment();
+        $comment->setCreatedAtValue();
+        $context = [];
+
+        $response = new MockResponse('', ['response_headers' => ['x-akismet-
pro-tip: discard']]);
+        yield 'blatant_spam' => [2, $response, $comment, $context];
+
+        $response = new MockResponse('true');
+        yield 'spam' => [1, $response, $comment, $context];
+
+        $response = new MockResponse('false');
+        yield 'ham' => [0, $response, $comment, $context];
+    }
 }
```

PHPUnit data providers allow us to reuse the same test logic for several
test cases.

17.2 Writing Functional Tests for Controllers

Testing controllers is a bit different than testing a "regular" PHP class as
we want to run them in the context of an HTTP request.

Install some extra dependencies needed for functional tests:

```
$ symfony composer require browser-kit --dev
```

Create a functional test for the Conference controller:

tests/Controller/ConferenceControllerTest.php
```
namespace App\Tests\Controller;

use Symfony\Bundle\FrameworkBundle\Test\WebTestCase;

class ConferenceControllerTest extends WebTestCase
{
    public function testIndex()
    {
```

```
$client = static::createClient();
$client->request('GET', '/');

$this->assertResponseIsSuccessful();
$this->assertSelectorTextContains('h2', 'Give your feedback');
    }
}
```

This first test checks that the homepage returns a 200 HTTP response.

The `$client` variable simulates a browser. Instead of making HTTP calls to the server though, it calls the Symfony application directly. This strategy has several benefits: it is much faster than having round-trips between the client and the server, but it also allows the tests to introspect the state of the services after each HTTP request.

Assertions such as `assertResponseIsSuccessful` are added on top of PHPUnit to ease your work. There are many such assertions defined by Symfony.

We have used / for the URL instead of generating it via the router. This is done on purpose as testing end-user URLs is part of what we want to test. If you change the route path, tests will break as a nice reminder that you should probably redirect the old URL to the new one to be nice with search engines and websites that link back to your website.

We could have generated the test via the maker bundle:

```
$ symfony console make:functional-test Controller\\ConferenceController
```

PHPUnit tests are executed in a dedicated **test** environment. We must set the `AKISMET_KEY` secret for this environment:

```
$ APP_ENV=test symfony console secrets:set AKISMET_KEY
```

Run the new tests only by passing the path to their class:

```
$ symfony php bin/phpunit tests/Controller/ConferenceControllerTest.php
```

When a test fails, it might be useful to introspect the Response object. Access it via `$client->getResponse()` and `echo` it to see what it looks like.

17.3 Defining Fixtures

To be able to test the comment list, the pagination, and the form submission, we need to populate the database with some data. And we want the data to be the same between test runs to make the tests pass. Fixtures are exactly what we need.

Install the Doctrine Fixtures bundle:

```
$ symfony composer req orm-fixtures --dev
```

A new **src/DataFixtures/** directory has been created during the installation with a sample class, ready to be customized. Add two conferences and one comment for now:

```
--- a/src/DataFixtures/AppFixtures.php
+++ b/src/DataFixtures/AppFixtures.php
@@ -2,6 +2,8 @@

 namespace App\DataFixtures;

+use App\Entity\Comment;
+use App\Entity\Conference;
 use Doctrine\Bundle\FixturesBundle\Fixture;
 use Doctrine\Common\Persistence\ObjectManager;

@@ -9,8 +11,24 @@ class AppFixtures extends Fixture
 {
     public function load(ObjectManager $manager)
     {
-        // $product = new Product();
-        // $manager->persist($product);
+        $amsterdam = new Conference();
+        $amsterdam->setCity('Amsterdam');
+        $amsterdam->setYear('2019');
+        $amsterdam->setIsInternational(true);
+        $manager->persist($amsterdam);
+
+        $paris = new Conference();
+        $paris->setCity('Paris');
+        $paris->setYear('2020');
+        $paris->setIsInternational(false);
+        $manager->persist($paris);
+
+        $comment1 = new Comment();
+        $comment1->setConference($amsterdam);
+        $comment1->setAuthor('Fabien');
+        $comment1->setEmail('fabien@example.com');
+        $comment1->setText('This was a great conference.');
+        $manager->persist($comment1);

         $manager->flush();
     }
}
```

When we will load the fixtures, all data will be removed; including the admin user. To avoid that, let's add the admin user in the fixtures:

```
--- a/src/DataFixtures/AppFixtures.php
+++ b/src/DataFixtures/AppFixtures.php
@@ -2,13 +2,22 @@

 namespace App\DataFixtures;

+use App\Entity\Admin;
 use App\Entity\Comment;
 use App\Entity\Conference;
 use Doctrine\Bundle\FixturesBundle\Fixture;
 use Doctrine\Common\Persistence\ObjectManager;
+use Symfony\Component\Security\Core\Encoder\EncoderFactoryInterface;

 class AppFixtures extends Fixture
 {
+    private $encoderFactory;
+
+    public function __construct(EncoderFactoryInterface $encoderFactory)
+    {
+        $this->encoderFactory = $encoderFactory;
+    }
+
     public function load(ObjectManager $manager)
     {
         $amsterdam = new Conference();
@@ -30,6 +39,12 @@ class AppFixtures extends Fixture
         $comment1->setText('This was a great conference.');
         $manager->persist($comment1);

+        $admin = new Admin();
+        $admin->setRoles(['ROLE_ADMIN']);
+        $admin->setUsername('admin');
+        $admin->setPassword($this->encoderFactory->getEncoder(Admin::class)->encodePassword('admin', null));
+        $manager->persist($admin);
+
         $manager->flush();
     }
 }
```

 If you don't remember which service you need to use for a given task, use the `debug:autowiring` with some keyword:

```
$ symfony console debug:autowiring encoder
```

17.4 Loading Fixtures

Load the fixtures into the database. **Be warned** that it will delete *all* data currently stored in the database (if you want to avoid this behavior, keep reading).

```
$ symfony console doctrine:fixtures:load
```

17.5 Crawling a Website in Functional Tests

As we have seen, the HTTP client used in the tests simulates a browser, so we can navigate through the website as if we were using a headless browser.

Add a new test that clicks on a conference page from the homepage:

```
--- a/tests/Controller/ConferenceControllerTest.php
+++ b/tests/Controller/ConferenceControllerTest.php
@@ -14,4 +14,19 @@ class ConferenceControllerTest extends WebTestCase
         $this->assertResponseIsSuccessful();
         $this->assertSelectorTextContains('h2', 'Give your feedback');
     }
+
+    public function testConferencePage()
+    {
+        $client = static::createClient();
+        $crawler = $client->request('GET', '/');
+
+        $this->assertCount(2, $crawler->filter('h4'));
+
+        $client->clickLink('View');
+
+        $this->assertPageTitleContains('Amsterdam');
+        $this->assertResponseIsSuccessful();
+        $this->assertSelectorTextContains('h2', 'Amsterdam 2019');
+        $this->assertSelectorExists('div:contains("There are 1 comments")');
+    }
 }
```

Let's describe what happens in this test in plain English:

- Like the first test, we go to the homepage;

- The `request()` method returns a `Crawler` instance that helps find elements on the page (like links, forms, or anything you can reach with CSS selectors or XPath);

- Thanks to a CSS selector, we assert that we have two conferences listed on the homepage;

- We then click on the "View" link (as it cannot click on more than one link at a time, Symfony automatically chooses the first one it finds);

- We assert the page title, the response, and the page `<h2>` to be sure we are on the right page (we could also have checked for the route that matches);

- Finally, we assert that there is 1 comment on the page. `div:contains()` is not a valid CSS selector, but Symfony has some nice additions, borrowed from jQuery.

Instead of clicking on text (i.e. `View`), we could have selected the link via a CSS selector as well:

```
$client->click($crawler->filter('h4 + p a')->link());
```

Check that the new test is green:

```
$ symfony php bin/phpunit tests/Controller/ConferenceControllerTest.php
```

17.6 Working with a Test Database

By default, tests are run in the `test` Symfony environment as defined in the `phpunit.xml.dist` file:

phpunit.xml.dist
```
<phpunit>
    <php>
        <server name="APP_ENV" value="test" force="true" />
    </php>
</phpunit>
```

If you want to use a different database for your tests, override the `DATABASE_URL` environment variable in the `.env.test` file:

```
--- a/.env.test
+++ b/.env.test
@@ -1,4 +1,5 @@
 # define your env variables for the test env here
+DATABASE_URL=postgres://main:main@127.0.0.1:32773/
test?sslmode=disable&charset=utf8
 KERNEL_CLASS='App\Kernel'
 APP_SECRET='$ecretf0rt3st'
 SYMFONY_DEPRECATIONS_HELPER=999999
```

Load the fixtures for the `test` environment/database:

```
$ APP_ENV=test symfony console doctrine:fixtures:load
```

For the rest of this step, we won't redefine the `DATABASE_URL` environment variable. Using the same database as the `dev` environment for tests has some advantages we will see in the next section.

17.7 Submitting a Form in a Functional Test

Do you want to get to the next level? Try adding a new comment with a photo on a conference from a test by simulating a form submission. That seems ambitious, doesn't it? Look at the needed code: not more complex than what we already wrote:

```
--- a/tests/Controller/ConferenceControllerTest.php
+++ b/tests/Controller/ConferenceControllerTest.php
@@ -29,4 +29,19 @@ class ConferenceControllerTest extends WebTestCase
         $this->assertSelectorTextContains('h2', 'Amsterdam 2019');
         $this->assertSelectorExists('div:contains("There are 1 comments")');
     }
+
+    public function testCommentSubmission()
+    {
+        $client = static::createClient();
+        $client->request('GET', '/conference/amsterdam-2019');
+        $client->submitForm('Submit', [
+            'comment_form[author]' => 'Fabien',
+            'comment_form[text]' => 'Some feedback from an automated
functional test',
+            'comment_form[email]' => 'me@automat.ed',
+            'comment_form[photo]' => dirname(__DIR__, 2).'/public/images/
under-construction.gif',
+        ]);
+        $this->assertResponseRedirects();
+        $client->followRedirect();
+        $this->assertSelectorExists('div:contains("There are 2 comments")');
+    }
 }
```

To submit a form via `submitForm()`, find the input names thanks to the browser DevTools or via the Symfony Profiler Form panel. Note the clever re-use of the under construction image!

Run the tests again to check that everything is green:

```
$ symfony php bin/phpunit tests/Controller/ConferenceControllerTest.php
```

One advantage of using the "dev" database for tests is that you can check the result in a browser:

17.8 Reloading the Fixtures

If you run the tests a second time, they should fail. As there are now more comments in the database, the assertion that checks the number of comments is broken. We need to reset the state of the database between each run by reloading the fixtures before each run:

```
$ symfony console doctrine:fixtures:load
$ symfony php bin/phpunit tests/Controller/ConferenceControllerTest.php
```

17.9 Automating your Workflow with a Makefile

Having to remember a sequence of commands to run the tests is annoying. This should at least be documented. But documentation should be a last resort. Instead, what about automating day to day activities? That would serve as documentation, help discovery by other developers, and make developer lives easier and fast.

Using a Makefile is one way to automate commands:

Makefile
```
SHELL := /bin/bash

tests:
    symfony console doctrine:fixtures:load -n
    symfony php bin/phpunit
.PHONY: tests
```

Note the -n flag on the Doctrine command; it is a global flag on Symfony commands that makes them non interactive.

Whenever you want to run the tests, use `make tests`:

```
$ make tests
```

17.10 Resetting the Database after each Test

Resetting the database after each test run is nice, but having truly independent tests is even better. We don't want one test to rely on the results of the previous ones. Changing the order of the tests should not change the outcome. As we're going to figure out now, this is not the case for the moment.

Move the `testConferencePage` test after the `testCommentSubmission` one:

```
--- a/tests/Controller/ConferenceControllerTest.php
+++ b/tests/Controller/ConferenceControllerTest.php
@@ -15,21 +15,6 @@ class ConferenceControllerTest extends WebTestCase
         $this->assertSelectorTextContains('h2', 'Give your feedback');
     }

-    public function testConferencePage()
-    {
-        $client = static::createClient();
-        $crawler = $client->request('GET', '/');
-
-        $this->assertCount(2, $crawler->filter('h4'));
-
-        $client->clickLink('View');
-
-        $this->assertPageTitleContains('Amsterdam');
-        $this->assertResponseIsSuccessful();
-        $this->assertSelectorTextContains('h2', 'Amsterdam 2019');
-        $this->assertSelectorExists('div:contains("There are 1 comments")');
-    }
-
     public function testCommentSubmission()
     {
         $client = static::createClient();
@@ -44,4 +29,19 @@ class ConferenceControllerTest extends WebTestCase
         $crawler = $client->followRedirect();
         $this->assertSelectorExists('div:contains("There are 2 comments")');
     }
+
+    public function testConferencePage()
+    {
+        $client = static::createClient();
+        $crawler = $client->request('GET', '/');
+
```

```
+            $this->assertCount(2, $crawler->filter('h4'));
+
+            $client->clickLink('View');
+
+            $this->assertPageTitleContains('Amsterdam');
+            $this->assertResponseIsSuccessful();
+            $this->assertSelectorTextContains('h2', 'Amsterdam 2019');
+            $this->assertSelectorExists('div:contains("There are 1 comments")');
+    }
 }
```

Tests now fail.

To reset the database between tests, install DoctrineTestBundle:

```
$ symfony composer require dama/doctrine-test-bundle --dev
```

You will need to confirm the execution of the recipe (as it is not an "officially" supported bundle):

```
Symfony operations: 1 recipe (d7f110145ba9f62430d1ad64d57ab069)
  -  WARNING  dama/doctrine-test-bundle (>=4.0): From github.com/symfony/
recipes-contrib:master
     The recipe for this package comes from the "contrib" repository, which is
open to community contributions.
     Review the recipe at https://github.com/symfony/recipes-contrib/tree/
master/dama/doctrine-test-bundle/4.0

     Do you want to execute this recipe?
     [y] Yes
     [n] No
     [a] Yes for all packages, only for the current installation session
     [p] Yes permanently, never ask again for this project
     (defaults to n): p
```

Enable the PHPUnit listener:

```
--- a/phpunit.xml.dist
+++ b/phpunit.xml.dist
@@ -27,6 +27,10 @@
         </whitelist>
     </filter>

+    <extensions>
+        <extension class="DAMA\DoctrineTestBundle\PHPUnit\PHPUnitExtension" />
+    </extensions>
+
     <listeners>
         <listener class="Symfony\Bridge\PhpUnit\SymfonyTestsListener" />
     </listeners>
```

And done. Any changes done in tests are now automatically rolled-back at the end of each test.

Tests should be green again:

```
$ make tests
```

17.11 Using a real Browser for Functional Tests

Functional tests use a special browser that calls the Symfony layer directly. But you can also use a real browser and the real HTTP layer thanks to Symfony Panther:

 At the time I wrote this paragraph, it was not possible to install Panther on a Symfony 5 project as one dependency was not compatible yet.

```
$ symfony composer req panther --dev
```

You can then write tests that use a real Google Chrome browser with the following changes:

```
--- a/tests/Controller/ConferenceControllerTest.php
+++ b/tests/Controller/ConferenceControllerTest.php
@@ -2,13 +2,13 @@

 namespace App\Tests\Controller;

-use Symfony\Bundle\FrameworkBundle\Test\WebTestCase;
+use Symfony\Component\Panther\PantherTestCase;

-class ConferenceControllerTest extends WebTestCase
+class ConferenceControllerTest extends PantherTestCase
 {
     public function testIndex()
     {
-        $client = static::createClient();
+        $client = static::createPantherClient(['external_base_uri' =>
$_SERVER['SYMFONY_DEFAULT_ROUTE_URL']]);
         $client->request('GET', '/');

         $this->assertResponseIsSuccessful();
```

The `SYMFONY_DEFAULT_ROUTE_URL` environment variable contains the URL of the local web server.

17.12 Running Black Box Functional Tests with

Blackfire

Another way to run functional tests is to use the *Blackfire player*[1]. In addition to what you can do with functional tests, it can also perform performance tests.

Refer to the step about "Performance" to learn more.

 Going Further

- *List of assertions defined by Symfony*[2] for functional tests;
- *PHPUnit docs*[3];
- The *Faker library*[4] to generate realistic fixtures data;
- The *CssSelector component docs*[5];
- The *Symfony Panther*[6] library for browser testing and web crawling in Symfony applications;
- The *Make/Makefile docs*[7].

1. https://blackfire.io/player
2. https://symfony.com/doc/current/testing/functional_tests_assertions.html
3. https://phpunit.de/documentation.html
4. https://github.com/fzaninotto/Faker
5. https://symfony.com/doc/current/components/css_selector.html
6. https://github.com/symfony/panther
7. https://www.gnu.org/software/make/manual/make.html

Step 18

Going Async

Checking for spam during the handling of the form submission might lead to some problems. If the Akismet API becomes slow, our website will also be slow for users. But even worse, if we hit a timeout or if the Akismet API is unavailable, we might lose comments.

Ideally, we should store the submitted data without publishing it, and immediately return a response. Checking for spam can then be done out of band.

18.1 Flagging Comments

We need to introduce a `state` for comments: `submitted`, `spam`, and `published`.

Add the `state` property to the `Comment` class:

```
$ symfony console make:entity Comment
```

Create a database migration:

```
$ symfony console make:migration
```

Modify the migration to update all existing comments to be `published` by default:

```
--- a/migrations/Version00000000000000.php
+++ b/migrations/Version00000000000000.php
@@ -20,7 +20,9 @@ final class Version20200714155905 extends AbstractMigration
     public function up(Schema $schema) : void
     {
         // this up() migration is auto-generated, please modify it to your
needs
-        $this->addSql('ALTER TABLE comment ADD state VARCHAR(255) NOT NULL');
+        $this->addSql('ALTER TABLE comment ADD state VARCHAR(255)');
+        $this->addSql("UPDATE comment SET state='published'");
+        $this->addSql('ALTER TABLE comment ALTER COLUMN state SET NOT NULL');
     }

     public function down(Schema $schema) : void
```

Migrate the database:

```
$ symfony console doctrine:migrations:migrate
```

We should also make sure that, by default, the state is set to submitted:

```
--- a/src/Entity/Comment.php
+++ b/src/Entity/Comment.php
@@ -49,9 +49,9 @@ class Comment
     private $photoFilename;

     /**
-     * @ORM\Column(type="string", length=255)
+     * @ORM\Column(type="string", length=255, options={"default":
"submitted"})
     */
-    private $state;
+    private $state = 'submitted';

     public function __toString(): string
     {
```

Update the EasyAdmin configuration to be able to see the comment's state:

```
--- a/config/packages/easy_admin.yaml
+++ b/config/packages/easy_admin.yaml
@@ -18,6 +18,7 @@ easy_admin:
                     - author
                     - { property: 'email', type: 'email' }
                     - { property: 'photoFilename', type: 'image',
'base_path': "/uploads/photos", label: 'Photo' }
+                    - state
                     - { property: 'createdAt', type: 'datetime' }
                 sort: ['createdAt', 'ASC']
                 filters: ['conference']
@@ -26,5 +27,6 @@ easy_admin:
                     - { property: 'conference' }
```

```
                        - { property: 'createdAt', type: datetime, type_options:
{ attr: { readonly: true } } }
                        - 'author'
+                       - { property: 'state' }
                        - { property: 'email', type: 'email' }
                        - text
```

Don't forget to also update the tests by setting the **state** of the fixtures:

```
--- a/src/DataFixtures/AppFixtures.php
+++ b/src/DataFixtures/AppFixtures.php
@@ -37,8 +37,16 @@ class AppFixtures extends Fixture
        $comment1->setAuthor('Fabien');
        $comment1->setEmail('fabien@example.com');
        $comment1->setText('This was a great conference.');
+       $comment1->setState('published');
        $manager->persist($comment1);

+       $comment2 = new Comment();
+       $comment2->setConference($amsterdam);
+       $comment2->setAuthor('Lucas');
+       $comment2->setEmail('lucas@example.com');
+       $comment2->setText('I think this one is going to be moderated.');
+       $manager->persist($comment2);
+
        $admin = new Admin();
        $admin->setRoles(['ROLE_ADMIN']);
        $admin->setUsername('admin');
```

For the controller tests, simulate the validation:

```
--- a/tests/Controller/ConferenceControllerTest.php
+++ b/tests/Controller/ConferenceControllerTest.php
@@ -2,6 +2,8 @@

 namespace App\Tests\Controller;

+use App\Repository\CommentRepository;
+use Doctrine\ORM\EntityManagerInterface;
 use Symfony\Bundle\FrameworkBundle\Test\WebTestCase;

 class ConferenceControllerTest extends WebTestCase
@@ -22,11 +24,17 @@ class ConferenceControllerTest extends WebTestCase
        $client->submitForm('Submit', [
            'comment_form[author]' => 'Fabien',
            'comment_form[text]' => 'Some feedback from an automated
functional test',
-           'comment_form[email]' => 'me@automat.ed',
+           'comment_form[email]' => $email = 'me@automat.ed',
            'comment_form[photo]' => dirname(__DIR__, 2).'/public/images/
under-construction.gif',
        ]);
        $this->assertResponseRedirects();
+
```

```
+          // simulate comment validation
+          $comment = self::$container->get(CommentRepository::class)-
>findOneByEmail($email);
+          $comment->setState('published');
+          self::$container->get(EntityManagerInterface::class)->flush();
+
           $client->followRedirect();
           $this->assertSelectorExists('div:contains("There are 2 comments")');
       }
```

From a PHPUnit test, you can get any service from the container via
self::$container->get(); it also gives access to non-public services.

18.2 Understanding Messenger

Managing asynchronous code with Symfony is the job of the Messenger
Component:

```
$ symfony composer req messenger
```

When some logic should be executed asynchronously, send a *message*
to a *messenger bus*. The bus stores the message in a *queue* and returns
immediately to let the flow of operations resume as fast as possible.

A *consumer* runs continuously in the background to read new messages
on the queue and execute the associated logic. The consumer can run on
the same server as the web application or on a separate one.

It is very similar to the way HTTP requests are handled, except that we
don't have responses.

18.3 Coding a Message Handler

A message is a data object class that should not hold any logic. It will be
serialized to be stored in a queue, so only store "simple" serializable data.

Create the CommentMessage class:

src/Message/CommentMessage.php
```
namespace App\Message;

class CommentMessage
{
    private $id;
    private $context;
```

```
    public function __construct(int $id, array $context = [])
    {
        $this->id = $id;
        $this->context = $context;
    }

    public function getId(): int
    {
        return $this->id;
    }

    public function getContext(): array
    {
        return $this->context;
    }
}
```

In the Messenger world, we don't have controllers, but message handlers.

Create a `CommentMessageHandler` class under a new `App\MessageHandler` namespace that knows how to handle `CommentMessage` messages:

src/MessageHandler/CommentMessageHandler.php
```
namespace App\MessageHandler;

use App\Message\CommentMessage;
use App\Repository\CommentRepository;
use App\SpamChecker;
use Doctrine\ORM\EntityManagerInterface;
use Symfony\Component\Messenger\Handler\MessageHandlerInterface;

class CommentMessageHandler implements MessageHandlerInterface
{
    private $spamChecker;
    private $entityManager;
    private $commentRepository;

    public function __construct(EntityManagerInterface $entityManager,
SpamChecker $spamChecker, CommentRepository $commentRepository)
    {
        $this->entityManager = $entityManager;
        $this->spamChecker = $spamChecker;
        $this->commentRepository = $commentRepository;
    }

    public function __invoke(CommentMessage $message)
    {
        $comment = $this->commentRepository->find($message->getId());
        if (!$comment) {
            return;
        }

        if (2 === $this->spamChecker->getSpamScore($comment,
```

```
$message->getContext())) {
            $comment->setState('spam');
        } else {
            $comment->setState('published');
        }

        $this->entityManager->flush();
    }
}
```

MessageHandlerInterface is a *marker* interface. It only helps Symfony auto-register and auto-configure the class as a Messenger handler. By convention, the logic of a handler lives in a method called __invoke(). The CommentMessage type hint on this method's one argument tells Messenger which class this will handle.

Update the controller to use the new system:

```
--- a/src/Controller/ConferenceController.php
+++ b/src/Controller/ConferenceController.php
@@ -5,14 +5,15 @@ namespace App\Controller;
 use App\Entity\Comment;
 use App\Entity\Conference;
 use App\Form\CommentFormType;
+use App\Message\CommentMessage;
 use App\Repository\CommentRepository;
 use App\Repository\ConferenceRepository;
-use App\SpamChecker;
 use Doctrine\ORM\EntityManagerInterface;
 use Symfony\Bundle\FrameworkBundle\Controller\AbstractController;
 use Symfony\Component\HttpFoundation\File\Exception\FileException;
 use Symfony\Component\HttpFoundation\Request;
 use Symfony\Component\HttpFoundation\Response;
+use Symfony\Component\Messenger\MessageBusInterface;
 use Symfony\Component\Routing\Annotation\Route;
 use Twig\Environment;

@@ -20,11 +21,13 @@ class ConferenceController extends AbstractController
 {
     private $twig;
     private $entityManager;
+    private $bus;

-    public function __construct(Environment $twig, EntityManagerInterface $entityManager)
+    public function __construct(Environment $twig, EntityManagerInterface $entityManager, MessageBusInterface $bus)
     {
         $this->twig = $twig;
         $this->entityManager = $entityManager;
+        $this->bus = $bus;
     }

     /**
```

```
@@ -40,7 +43,7 @@ class ConferenceController extends AbstractController
     /**
      * @Route("/conference/{slug}", name="conference")
      */
-    public function show(Request $request, Conference $conference,
CommentRepository $commentRepository, SpamChecker $spamChecker, string
$photoDir)
+    public function show(Request $request, Conference $conference,
CommentRepository $commentRepository, string $photoDir)
     {
         $comment = new Comment();
         $form = $this->createForm(CommentFormType::class, $comment);
@@ -59,6 +62,7 @@ class ConferenceController extends AbstractController
         }

             $this->entityManager->persist($comment);
+            $this->entityManager->flush();

             $context = [
                 'user_ip' => $request->getClientIp(),
@@ -66,11 +70,8 @@ class ConferenceController extends AbstractController
                 'referrer' => $request->headers->get('referer'),
                 'permalink' => $request->getUri(),
             ];
-            if (2 === $spamChecker->getSpamScore($comment, $context)) {
-                throw new \RuntimeException('Blatant spam, go away!');
-            }

-            $this->entityManager->flush();
+            $this->bus->dispatch(new CommentMessage($comment->getId(),
$context));

             return $this->redirectToRoute('conference', ['slug' =>
$conference->getSlug()]);
         }
```

Instead of depending on the Spam Checker, we now dispatch a message on the bus. The handler then decides what to do with it.

We have achieved something unexpected. We have decoupled our controller from the Spam Checker and moved the logic to a new class, the handler. It is a perfect use case for the bus. Test the code, it works. Everything is still done synchronously, but the code is probably already "better".

18.4 Restricting Displayed Comments

Update the display logic to avoid non-published comments from appearing on the frontend:

```
--- a/src/Repository/CommentRepository.php
+++ b/src/Repository/CommentRepository.php
@@ -25,7 +25,9 @@ class CommentRepository extends ServiceEntityRepository
     {
         return $this->createQueryBuilder('c')
             ->andWhere('c.conference = :conference')
+            ->andWhere('c.state = :state')
             ->setParameter('conference', $conference)
+            ->setParameter('state', 'published')
             ->orderBy('c.createdAt', 'DESC')
             ->setMaxResults($limit)
             ->setFirstResult($offset)
```

18.5 Going Async for Real

By default, handlers are called synchronously. To go async, you need to explicitly configure which queue to use for each handler in the `config/packages/messenger.yaml` configuration file:

```
--- a/config/packages/messenger.yaml
+++ b/config/packages/messenger.yaml
@@ -5,10 +5,10 @@ framework:

        transports:
            # https://symfony.com/doc/current/messenger.html#transport-
configuration
-            # async: '%env(MESSENGER_TRANSPORT_DSN)%'
+            async: '%env(RABBITMQ_DSN)%'
            # failed: 'doctrine://default?queue_name=failed'
            # sync: 'sync://'

        routing:
            # Route your messages to the transports
-            # 'App\Message\YourMessage': async
+            App\Message\CommentMessage: async
```

The configuration tells the bus to send instances of `App\Message\CommentMessage` to the `async` queue, which is defined by a DSN, stored in the `RABBITMQ_DSN` environment variable.

18.6 Adding RabbitMQ to the Docker Stack

As you might have guessed, we are going to use RabbitMQ:

```
--- a/docker-compose.yaml
+++ b/docker-compose.yaml
```

```
@@ -12,3 +12,7 @@ services:
    redis:
        image: redis:5-alpine
        ports: [6379]
+
+    rabbitmq:
+        image: rabbitmq:3.7-management
+        ports: [5672, 15672]
```

18.7 Restarting Docker Services

To force Docker Compose to take the RabbitMQ container into account, stop the containers and restart them:

```
$ docker-compose stop
$ docker-compose up -d
```

Dumping and Restoring Database Data

Never call `docker-compose down` if you don't want to lose data. Or backup first. Use `pg_dump` to dump the database data:

```
$ symfony run pg_dump --data-only > dump.sql
```

And restore the data:

```
$ symfony run psql < dump.sql
```

18.8 Consuming Messages

If you try to submit a new comment, the spam checker won't be called anymore. Add an `error_log()` call in the `getSpamScore()` method to confirm. Instead, a message is waiting in RabbitMQ, ready to be consumed by some processes.

As you might imagine, Symfony comes with a consumer command. Run it now:

```
$ symfony console messenger:consume async -vv
```

It should immediately consume the message dispatched for the

169

submitted comment:

```
[OK] Consuming messages from transports "async".

// The worker will automatically exit once it has received a stop signal via
the messenger:stop-workers command.

// Quit the worker with CONTROL-C.
```

```
11:30:20 INFO       [messenger] Received message App\Message\CommentMessage
["message" => App\Message\CommentMessage^ { …},"class" => "App\Message\
CommentMessage"]
11:30:20 INFO       [http_client] Request: "POST
https://80cea32be1f6.rest.akismet.com/1.1/comment-check"
11:30:20 INFO       [http_client] Response: "200
https://80cea32be1f6.rest.akismet.com/1.1/comment-check"
11:30:20 INFO       [messenger] Message App\Message\CommentMessage handled by
App\MessageHandler\CommentMessageHandler::__invoke ["message" => App\Message\
CommentMessage^ { …},"class" => "App\Message\CommentMessage","handler" => "App\
MessageHandler\CommentMessageHandler::__invoke"]
11:30:20 INFO       [messenger] App\Message\CommentMessage was handled
successfully (acknowledging to transport). ["message" => App\Message\
CommentMessage^ { …},"class" => "App\Message\CommentMessage"]
```

The message consumer activity is logged, but you get instant feedback on the console by passing the -vv flag. You should even be able to spot the call to the Akismet API.

To stop the consumer, press Ctrl+C.

18.9 Exploring the RabbitMQ Web Management Interface

If you want to see queues and messages flowing through RabbitMQ, open its web management interface:

```
$ symfony open:local:rabbitmq
```

Or from the web debug toolbar:

Use guest/guest to login to the RabbitMQ management UI:

18.10 Running Workers in the Background

Instead of launching the consumer every time we post a comment and stopping it immediately after, we want to run it continuously without having too many terminal windows or tabs open.

The Symfony CLI can manage such background commands or workers by using the daemon flag (-d) on the run command.

Run the message consumer again, but send it in the background:

```
$ symfony run -d --watch=config,src,templates,vendor symfony console
messenger:consume async
```

The --watch option tells Symfony that the command must be restarted whenever there is a filesystem change in the config/, src/, templates/, or vendor/ directories.

 Do not use -vv as you would have duplicated messages in server:log (logged messages and console messages).

If the consumer stops working for some reason (memory limit, bug, ...), it will be restarted automatically. And if the consumer fails too fast, the Symfony CLI will give up.

Logs are streamed via symfony server:log with all the other logs coming from PHP, the web server, and the application:

```
$ symfony server:log
```

Use the server:status command to list all background workers managed for the current project:

```
$ symfony server:status
```

```
Web server listening on https://127.0.0.1:8000
  Command symfony console messenger:consume async running with PID 15774
(watching config/, src/, templates/)
```

To stop a worker, stop the web server or kill the PID given by the server:status command:

```
$ kill 15774
```

18.11 Retrying Failed Messages

What if Akismet is down while consuming a message? There is no impact for people submitting comments, but the message is lost and spam is not checked.

Messenger has a retry mechanism for when an exception occurs while handling a message. Let's configure it:

```
--- a/config/packages/messenger.yaml
+++ b/config/packages/messenger.yaml
@@ -5,10 +5,17 @@ framework:

        transports:
            # https://symfony.com/doc/current/messenger.html#transport-
configuration
-           async: '%env(RABBITMQ_DSN)%'
-           # failed: 'doctrine://default?queue_name=failed'
+           async:
+               dsn: '%env(RABBITMQ_DSN)%'
+               retry_strategy:
+                   max_retries: 3
+                   multiplier: 2
+
+           failed: 'doctrine://default?queue_name=failed'
            # sync: 'sync://'

+       failure_transport: failed
+
        routing:
            # Route your messages to the transports
            App\Message\CommentMessage: async
```

If a problem occurs while handling a message, the consumer will retry 3 times before giving up. But instead of discarding the message, it will store it in a more permanent storage, the `failed` queue, which uses the Doctrine database.

Inspect failed messages and retry them via the following commands:

```
$ symfony console messenger:failed:show
```

```
$ symfony console messenger:failed:retry
```

18.12 Deploying RabbitMQ

Adding RabbitMQ to the production servers can be done by adding it to the list of services:

```
--- a/.symfony/services.yaml
+++ b/.symfony/services.yaml
@@ -5,3 +5,8 @@ db:

 rediscache:
     type: redis:5.0
+
+queue:
+    type: rabbitmq:3.7
+    disk: 1024
```

```
+    size: S
```

Reference it in the web container configuration as well and enable the amqp PHP extension:

```
--- a/.symfony.cloud.yaml
+++ b/.symfony.cloud.yaml
@@ -4,6 +4,7 @@ type: php:7.4

 runtime:
     extensions:
+        - amqp
         - pdo_pgsql
         - apcu
         - mbstring
@@ -22,6 +23,7 @@ variables:
 relationships:
     database: "db:postgresql"
     redis: "rediscache:redis"
+    rabbitmq: "queue:rabbitmq"

 web:
     locations:
```

When the RabbitMQ service is installed on a project, you can access its web management interface by opening the tunnel first:

```
$ symfony tunnel:open
$ symfony open:remote:rabbitmq

# when done
$ symfony tunnel:close
```

18.13 Running Workers on SymfonyCloud

To consume messages from RabbitMQ, we need to run the `messenger:consume` command continuously. On SymfonyCloud, this is the role of a *worker*:

```
--- a/.symfony.cloud.yaml
+++ b/.symfony.cloud.yaml
@@ -46,3 +46,12 @@ hooks:
         set -x -e

         (>&2 symfony-deploy)
+
+workers:
+    messages:
```

174

```
+        commands:
+            start: |
+                set -x -e
+
+                (>&2 symfony-deploy)
+                php bin/console messenger:consume async -vv --time-limit=3600
--memory-limit=128M
```

Like for the Symfony CLI, SymfonyCloud manages restarts and logs.
To get logs for a worker, use:

```
$ symfony logs --worker=messages all
```

 Going Further

- *SymfonyCasts Messenger tutorial*[1];
- The *Enterprise service bus*[2] architecture and the *CQRS pattern*[3];
- The *Symfony Messenger docs*[4];
- *RabbitMQ docs*[5].

1. https://symfonycasts.com/screencast/messenger
2. https://en.wikipedia.org/wiki/Enterprise_service_bus
3. https://martinfowler.com/bliki/CQRS.html
4. https://symfony.com/doc/current/messenger.html
5. https://www.rabbitmq.com/documentation.html

Step 19
Making Decisions with a Workflow

Having a state for a model is quite common. The comment state is only determined by the spam checker. What if we add more decision factors?

We might want to let the website admin moderate all comments after the spam checker. The process would be something along the lines of:

- Start with a `submitted` state when a comment is submitted by a user;

- Let the spam checker analyze the comment and switch the state to either `potential_spam`, `ham`, or `rejected`;

- If not rejected, wait for the website admin to decide if the comment is good enough by switching the state to `published` or `rejected`.

Implementing this logic is not too complex, but you can imagine that adding more rules would greatly increase the complexity. Instead of coding the logic ourselves, we can use the Symfony Workflow Component:

```
$ symfony composer req workflow
```

19.1 Describing Workflows

The comment workflow can be described in the `config/packages/workflow.yaml` file:

config/packages/workflow.yaml
```yaml
framework:
    workflows:
        comment:
            type: state_machine
            audit_trail:
                enabled: "%kernel.debug%"
            marking_store:
                type: 'method'
                property: 'state'
            supports:
                - App\Entity\Comment
            initial_marking: submitted
            places:
                - submitted
                - ham
                - potential_spam
                - spam
                - rejected
                - published
            transitions:
                accept:
                    from: submitted
                    to:   ham
                might_be_spam:
                    from: submitted
                    to:   potential_spam
                reject_spam:
                    from: submitted
                    to:   spam
                publish:
                    from: potential_spam
                    to:   published
                reject:
                    from: potential_spam
                    to:   rejected
                publish_ham:
                    from: ham
                    to:   published
                reject_ham:
                    from: ham
                    to:   rejected
```

To validate the workflow, generate a visual representation:

```
$ symfony console workflow:dump comment | dot -Tpng -o workflow.png
```

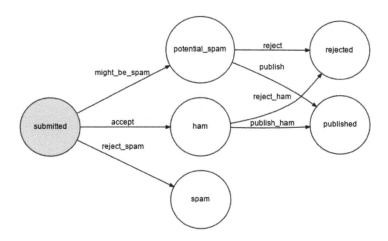

 The **dot** command is a part of the *Graphviz*[1] utility.

19.2 Using a Workflow

Replace the current logic in the message handler with the workflow:

```
--- a/src/MessageHandler/CommentMessageHandler.php
+++ b/src/MessageHandler/CommentMessageHandler.php
@@ -6,19 +6,28 @@ use App\Message\CommentMessage;
 use App\Repository\CommentRepository;
 use App\SpamChecker;
 use Doctrine\ORM\EntityManagerInterface;
+use Psr\Log\LoggerInterface;
 use Symfony\Component\Messenger\Handler\MessageHandlerInterface;
+use Symfony\Component\Messenger\MessageBusInterface;
+use Symfony\Component\Workflow\WorkflowInterface;

 class CommentMessageHandler implements MessageHandlerInterface
 {
     private $spamChecker;
     private $entityManager;
     private $commentRepository;
+    private $bus;
+    private $workflow;
+    private $logger;

-    public function __construct(EntityManagerInterface $entityManager,
SpamChecker $spamChecker, CommentRepository $commentRepository)
```

---

1. https://www.graphviz.org/

```
+    public function __construct(EntityManagerInterface $entityManager,
SpamChecker $spamChecker, CommentRepository $commentRepository,
MessageBusInterface $bus, WorkflowInterface $commentStateMachine,
LoggerInterface $logger = null)
     {
         $this->entityManager = $entityManager;
         $this->spamChecker = $spamChecker;
         $this->commentRepository = $commentRepository;
+        $this->bus = $bus;
+        $this->workflow = $commentStateMachine;
+        $this->logger = $logger;
     }

     public function __invoke(CommentMessage $message)
@@ -28,12 +37,21 @@ class CommentMessageHandler implements
MessageHandlerInterface
             return;
         }

-        if (2 === $this->spamChecker->getSpamScore($comment, $message-
>getContext())) {
-            $comment->setState('spam');
-        } else {
-            $comment->setState('published');
-        }
+
+        if ($this->workflow->can($comment, 'accept')) {
+            $score = $this->spamChecker->getSpamScore($comment, $message-
>getContext());
+            $transition = 'accept';
+            if (2 === $score) {
+                $transition = 'reject_spam';
+            } elseif (1 === $score) {
+                $transition = 'might_be_spam';
+            }
+            $this->workflow->apply($comment, $transition);
+            $this->entityManager->flush();

-        $this->entityManager->flush();
+            $this->bus->dispatch($message);
+        } elseif ($this->logger) {
+            $this->logger->debug('Dropping comment message', ['comment' =>
$comment->getId(), 'state' => $comment->getState()]);
+        }
     }
 }
```

The new logic reads as follows:

- If the accept transition is available for the comment in the message, check for spam;

- Depending on the outcome, choose the right transition to apply;

- Call apply() to update the Comment via a call to the setState() method;

- Call `flush()` to commit the changes to the database;
- Re-dispatch the message to allow the workflow to transition again.

As we haven't implemented the admin validation, the next time the message is consumed, the "Dropping comment message" will be logged.

Let's implement an auto-validation until the next chapter:

```
--- a/src/MessageHandler/CommentMessageHandler.php
+++ b/src/MessageHandler/CommentMessageHandler.php
@@ -47,6 +47,9 @@ class CommentMessageHandler implements
MessageHandlerInterface
            $this->entityManager->flush();

            $this->bus->dispatch($message);
+        } elseif ($this->workflow->can($comment, 'publish') || $this-
>workflow->can($comment, 'publish_ham')) {
+            $this->workflow->apply($comment, $this->workflow->can($comment,
'publish') ? 'publish' : 'publish_ham');
+            $this->entityManager->flush();
        } elseif ($this->logger) {
            $this->logger->debug('Dropping comment message', ['comment' =>
$comment->getId(), 'state' => $comment->getState()]);
        }
```

Run `symfony server:log` and add a comment in the frontend to see all transitions happening one after the other.

 ## Going Further

- *Workflows and State Machines*[2] and when to choose each one;
- The *Symfony Workflow docs*[3].

---

2. https://symfony.com/doc/current/workflow/workflow-and-state-machine.html
3. https://symfony.com/doc/current/workflow.html

Step 20
Emailing Admins

To ensure high quality feedback, the admin must moderate all comments. When a comment is in the ham or potential_spam state, an *email* should be sent to the admin with two links: one to accept the comment and one to reject it.

First, install the Symfony Mailer component:

```
$ symfony composer req mailer
```

20.1 Setting an Email for the Admin

To store the admin email, use a container parameter. For demonstration purpose, we also allow it to be set via an environment variable (should not be needed in "real life"). To ease injection in services that need the admin email, define a container bind setting:

```
--- a/config/services.yaml
+++ b/config/services.yaml
@@ -4,6 +4,7 @@
 # Put parameters here that don't need to change on each machine where the app
is deployed
 # https://symfony.com/doc/current/best_practices/
configuration.html#application-related-configuration
 parameters:
+    default_admin_email: admin@example.com
```

```
    services:
        # default configuration for services in *this* file
@@ -13,6 +14,7 @@ services:
            bind:
                $photoDir: "%kernel.project_dir%/public/uploads/photos"
                $akismetKey: "%env(AKISMET_KEY)%"
+                $adminEmail:
"%env(string:default:default_admin_email:ADMIN_EMAIL)%"

        # makes classes in src/ available to be used as services
        # this creates a service per class whose id is the fully-qualified class
name
```

An environment variable might be "processed" before being used. Here, we are using the default processor to fall back to the value of the default_admin_email parameter if the ADMIN_EMAIL environment variable does not exist.

20.2 Sending a Notification Email

To send an email, you can choose between several Email class abstractions; from Message, the lowest level, to NotificationEmail, the highest one. You will probably use the Email class the most, but NotificationEmail is the perfect choice for internal emails.

In the message handler, let's replace the auto-validation logic:

```
--- a/src/MessageHandler/CommentMessageHandler.php
+++ b/src/MessageHandler/CommentMessageHandler.php
@@ -7,6 +7,8 @@ use App\Repository\CommentRepository;
 use App\SpamChecker;
 use Doctrine\ORM\EntityManagerInterface;
 use Psr\Log\LoggerInterface;
+use Symfony\Bridge\Twig\Mime\NotificationEmail;
+use Symfony\Component\Mailer\MailerInterface;
 use Symfony\Component\Messenger\Handler\MessageHandlerInterface;
 use Symfony\Component\Messenger\MessageBusInterface;
 use Symfony\Component\Workflow\WorkflowInterface;
@@ -18,15 +20,19 @@ class CommentMessageHandler implements
MessageHandlerInterface
     private $commentRepository;
     private $bus;
     private $workflow;
+     private $mailer;
+     private $adminEmail;
     private $logger;

-     public function __construct(EntityManagerInterface $entityManager,
SpamChecker $spamChecker, CommentRepository $commentRepository,
MessageBusInterface $bus, WorkflowInterface $commentStateMachine,
```

```
LoggerInterface $logger = null)
+    public function __construct(EntityManagerInterface $entityManager,
SpamChecker $spamChecker, CommentRepository $commentRepository,
MessageBusInterface $bus, WorkflowInterface $commentStateMachine,
MailerInterface $mailer, string $adminEmail, LoggerInterface $logger = null)
    {
        $this->entityManager = $entityManager;
        $this->spamChecker = $spamChecker;
        $this->commentRepository = $commentRepository;
        $this->bus = $bus;
        $this->workflow = $commentStateMachine;
+       $this->mailer = $mailer;
+       $this->adminEmail = $adminEmail;
        $this->logger = $logger;
    }

@@ -51,8 +57,13 @@ class CommentMessageHandler implements
MessageHandlerInterface

            $this->bus->dispatch($message);
        } elseif ($this->workflow->can($comment, 'publish') || $this-
>workflow->can($comment, 'publish_ham')) {
-           $this->workflow->apply($comment, $this->workflow->can($comment,
'publish') ? 'publish' : 'publish_ham');
-           $this->entityManager->flush();
+           $this->mailer->send((new NotificationEmail())
+               ->subject('New comment posted')
+               ->htmlTemplate('emails/comment_notification.html.twig')
+               ->from($this->adminEmail)
+               ->to($this->adminEmail)
+               ->context(['comment' => $comment])
+           );
        } elseif ($this->logger) {
            $this->logger->debug('Dropping comment message', ['comment' =>
$comment->getId(), 'state' => $comment->getState()]);
        }
```

The `MailerInterface` is the main entry point and allows to `send()` emails.

To send an email, we need a sender (the `From`/`Sender` header). Instead of setting it explicitly on the Email instance, define it globally:

```
--- a/config/packages/mailer.yaml
+++ b/config/packages/mailer.yaml
@@ -1,3 +1,5 @@
 framework:
     mailer:
         dsn: '%env(MAILER_DSN)%'
+        envelope:
+            sender: "%env(string:default:default_admin_email:ADMIN_EMAIL)%"
```

185

20.3 Extending the Notification Email Template

The notification email template inherits from the default notification email template that comes with Symfony:

templates/emails/comment_notification.html.twig
```twig
{% extends '@email/default/notification/body.html.twig' %}

{% block content %}
    Author: {{ comment.author }}<br />
    Email: {{ comment.email }}<br />
    State: {{ comment.state }}<br />

    <p>
        {{ comment.text }}
    </p>
{% endblock %}

{% block action %}
    <spacer size="16"></spacer>
    <button href="{{ url('review_comment', { id: comment.id })
}}">Accept</button>
    <button href="{{ url('review_comment', { id: comment.id, reject: true })
}}">Reject</button>
{% endblock %}
```

The template overrides a few blocks to customize the message of the email and to add some links that allow the admin to accept or reject a comment. Any route argument that is not a valid route parameter is added as a query string item (the reject URL looks like /admin/comment/review/42?reject=true).

The default NotificationEmail template uses *Inky*[1] instead of HTML to design emails. It helps create responsive emails that are compatible with all popular email clients.

For maximum compatibility with email readers, the notification base layout inlines all stylesheets (via the CSS inliner package) by default.

These two features are part of optional Twig extensions that need to be installed:

```
$ symfony composer req twig/cssinliner-extra twig/inky-extra
```

20.4 Generating Absolute URLs in a Symfony

---

1. https://get.foundation/emails/docs/inky.html

Command

In emails, generate URLs with `url()` instead of `path()` as you need absolute ones (with scheme and host).

The email is sent from the message handler, in a console context. Generating absolute URLs in a Web context is easier as we know the scheme and domain of the current page. This is not the case in a console context.

Define the domain name and scheme to use explicitly:

```
--- a/config/services.yaml
+++ b/config/services.yaml
@@ -5,6 +5,11 @@
 # https://symfony.com/doc/current/best_practices/
configuration.html#application-related-configuration
 parameters:
     default_admin_email: admin@example.com
+    default_domain: '127.0.0.1'
+    default_scheme: 'http'
+
+    router.request_context.host:
'%env(default:default_domain:SYMFONY_DEFAULT_ROUTE_HOST)%'
+    router.request_context.scheme:
'%env(default:default_scheme:SYMFONY_DEFAULT_ROUTE_SCHEME)%'

 services:
     # default configuration for services in *this* file
```

The `SYMFONY_DEFAULT_ROUTE_HOST` and `SYMFONY_DEFAULT_ROUTE_PORT` environment variables are automatically set locally when using the `symfony` CLI and determined based on the configuration on SymfonyCloud.

20.5 Wiring a Route to a Controller

The `review_comment` route does not exist yet, let's create an admin controller to handle it:

src/Controller/AdminController.php
```php
namespace App\Controller;

use App\Entity\Comment;
use App\Message\CommentMessage;
use Doctrine\ORM\EntityManagerInterface;
use Symfony\Bundle\FrameworkBundle\Controller\AbstractController;
use Symfony\Component\HttpFoundation\Request;
use Symfony\Component\HttpFoundation\Response;
```

```php
use Symfony\Component\Messenger\MessageBusInterface;
use Symfony\Component\Routing\Annotation\Route;
use Symfony\Component\Workflow\Registry;
use Twig\Environment;

class AdminController extends AbstractController
{
    private $twig;
    private $entityManager;
    private $bus;

    public function __construct(Environment $twig, EntityManagerInterface
$entityManager, MessageBusInterface $bus)
    {
        $this->twig = $twig;
        $this->entityManager = $entityManager;
        $this->bus = $bus;
    }

    /**
     * @Route("/admin/comment/review/{id}", name="review_comment")
     */
    public function reviewComment(Request $request, Comment $comment, Registry
$registry)
    {
        $accepted = !$request->query->get('reject');

        $machine = $registry->get($comment);
        if ($machine->can($comment, 'publish')) {
            $transition = $accepted ? 'publish' : 'reject';
        } elseif ($machine->can($comment, 'publish_ham')) {
            $transition = $accepted ? 'publish_ham' : 'reject_ham';
        } else {
            return new Response('Comment already reviewed or not in the right
state.');
        }

        $machine->apply($comment, $transition);
        $this->entityManager->flush();

        if ($accepted) {
            $this->bus->dispatch(new CommentMessage($comment->getId()));
        }

        return $this->render('admin/review.html.twig', [
            'transition' => $transition,
            'comment' => $comment,
        ]);
    }
}
```

The review comment URL starts with /admin/ to protect it with the
firewall defined in a previous step. The admin needs to be authenticated
to access this resource.

Instead of creating a Response instance, we have used render(), a shortcut method provided by the `AbstractController` controller base class.

When the review is done, a short template thanks the admin for their hard work:

templates/admin/review.html.twig
```twig
{% extends 'base.html.twig' %}

{% block body %}
    <h2>Comment reviewed, thank you!</h2>

    <p>Applied transition: <strong>{{ transition }}</strong></p>
    <p>New state: <strong>{{ comment.state }}</strong></p>
{% endblock %}
```

20.6 Using a Mail Catcher

Instead of using a "real" SMTP server or a third-party provider to send emails, let's use a mail catcher. A mail catcher provides a SMTP server that does not deliver the emails, but makes them available through a Web interface instead:

```
--- a/docker-compose.yaml
+++ b/docker-compose.yaml
@@ -16,3 +16,7 @@ services:
     rabbitmq:
         image: rabbitmq:3.7-management
         ports: [5672, 15672]
+
+    mailer:
+        image: schickling/mailcatcher
+        ports: [1025, 1080]
```

Shut down and restart the containers to add the mail catcher:

```
$ docker-compose stop
$ docker-compose up -d
```

20.7 Accessing the Webmail

You can open the webmail from a terminal:

```
$ symfony open:local:webmail
```

Or from the web debug toolbar:

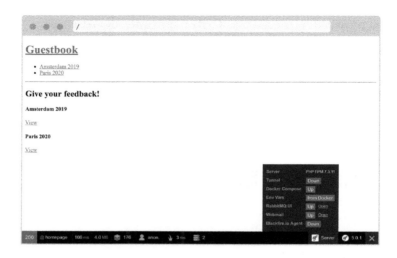

Submit a comment, you should receive an email in the webmail interface:

Click on the email title on the interface and accept or reject the comment as you see fit:

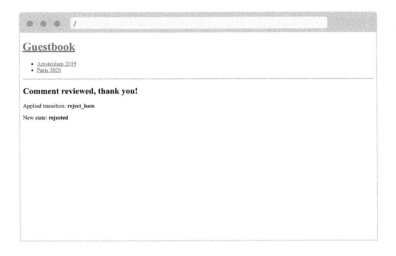

Check the logs with **server:log** if that does not work as expected.

20.8 Managing Long-Running Scripts

Having long-running scripts comes with behaviors that you should be aware of. Unlike the PHP model used for HTTP where each request starts with a clean state, the message consumer is running continuously in the background. Each handling of a message inherits the current state, including the memory cache. To avoid any issues with Doctrine, its entity managers are automatically cleared after the handling of a message. You should check if your own services need to do the same or not.

20.9 Sending Emails Asynchronously

The email sent in the message handler might take some time to be sent. It might even throw an exception. In case of an exception being thrown during the handling of a message, it will be retried. But instead of retrying to consume the comment message, it would be better to actually just retry sending the email.

We already know how to do that: send the email message on the bus.

A **MailerInterface** instance does the hard work: when a bus is defined, it dispatches the email messages on it instead of sending them. No changes are needed in your code.

But right now, the bus is sending the email synchronously as we have not configured the queue we want to use for emails. Let's use RabbitMQ again:

```
--- a/config/packages/messenger.yaml
+++ b/config/packages/messenger.yaml
@@ -19,3 +19,4 @@ framework:
         routing:
             # Route your messages to the transports
             App\Message\CommentMessage: async
+            Symfony\Component\Mailer\Messenger\SendEmailMessage: async
```

Even if we are using the same transport (RabbitMQ) for comment messages and email messages, it does not have to be the case. You could decide to use another transport to manage different message priorities for instance. Using different transports also gives you the opportunity to have different worker machines handling different kind of messages. It is flexible and up to you.

20.10 Testing Emails

There are many ways to test emails.

You can write unit tests if you write a class per email (by extending `Email` or `TemplatedEmail` for instance).

The most common tests you will write though are functional tests that check that some actions trigger an email, and probably tests about the content of the emails if they are dynamic.

Symfony comes with assertions that ease such tests:

```
public function testMailerAssertions()
{
    $client = static::createClient();
    $client->request('GET', '/');

    $this->assertEmailCount(1);
    $event = $this->getMailerEvent(0);
    $this->assertEmailIsQueued($event);

    $email = $this->getMailerMessage(0);
    $this->assertEmailHeaderSame($email, 'To', 'fabien@example.com');
    $this->assertEmailTextBodyContains($email, 'Bar');
    $this->assertEmailAttachmentCount($email, 1);
}
```

These assertions work when emails are sent synchronously or asynchronously.

20.11 Sending Emails on SymfonyCloud

There is no specific configuration for SymfonyCloud. All accounts come with a SendGrid account that is automatically used to send emails.

You still need to update the SymfonyCloud configuration to include the `xsl` PHP extension needed by Inky:

```
--- a/.symfony.cloud.yaml
+++ b/.symfony.cloud.yaml
@@ -4,6 +4,7 @@ type: php:7.3

 runtime:
     extensions:
+        - xsl
         - amqp
         - redis
         - pdo_pgsql
```

 To be on the safe side, emails are *only* sent on the `master` branch by default. Enable SMTP explicitly on non-`master` branches if you know what you are doing:

```
$ symfony env:setting:set email on
```

 ## Going Further

- *SymfonyCasts Mailer tutorial*[2];
- The *Inky templating language docs*[3];
- The *Environment Variable Processors*[4];
- The *Symfony Framework Mailer documentation*[5];
- The *SymfonyCloud documentation about Emails*[6].

---

2. https://symfonycasts.com/screencast/mailer
3. https://get.foundation/emails/docs/inky.html
4. https://symfony.com/doc/current/configuration/env_var_processors.html
5. https://symfony.com/doc/current/mailer.html
6. https://symfony.com/doc/master/cloud/services/emails.html

Step 21
Caching for Performance

Performance problems might come with popularity. Some typical examples: missing database indexes or tons of SQL requests per page. You won't have any problems with an empty database, but with more traffic and growing data, it might arise at some point.

21.1 Adding HTTP Cache Headers

Using HTTP caching strategies is a great way to maximize the performance for end users with little effort. Add a reverse proxy cache in production to enable caching, and use a CDN^1 to cache on the edge for even better performance.

Let's cache the homepage for an hour:

```
--- a/src/Controller/ConferenceController.php
+++ b/src/Controller/ConferenceController.php
@@ -37,9 +37,12 @@ class ConferenceController extends AbstractController
     */
    public function index(ConferenceRepository $conferenceRepository)
    {
-        return new Response($this->twig->render('conference/index.html.twig',
[
+        $response = new Response($this->twig->render('conference/
index.html.twig', [
            'conferences' => $conferenceRepository->findAll(),
```

---

1. https://en.wikipedia.org/wiki/Content_delivery_network

```
        ]));
+       $response->setSharedMaxAge(3600);
+
+       return $response;
    }

    /**
```

The `setSharedMaxAge()` method configures the cache expiration for reverse proxies. Use `setMaxAge()` to control the browser cache. Time is expressed in seconds (1 hour = 60 minutes = 3600 seconds).

Caching the conference page is more challenging as it is more dynamic. Anyone can add a comment anytime, and nobody wants to wait for an hour to see it online. In such cases, use the *HTTP validation* strategy.

21.2 Activating the Symfony HTTP Cache Kernel

To test the HTTP cache strategy, use the Symfony HTTP reverse proxy:

```
--- a/public/index.php
+++ b/public/index.php
@@ -1,6 +1,7 @@
 <?php

 use App\Kernel;
+use Symfony\Bundle\FrameworkBundle\HttpCache\HttpCache;
 use Symfony\Component\ErrorHandler\Debug;
 use Symfony\Component\HttpFoundation\Request;

@@ -21,6 +22,11 @@ if ($trustedHosts = $_SERVER['TRUSTED_HOSTS'] ??
$_ENV['TRUSTED_HOSTS'] ?? false
 }

 $kernel = new Kernel($_SERVER['APP_ENV'], (bool) $_SERVER['APP_DEBUG']);
+
+if ('dev' === $kernel->getEnvironment()) {
+    $kernel = new HttpCache($kernel);
+}
+
 $request = Request::createFromGlobals();
 $response = $kernel->handle($request);
 $response->send();
```

Besides being a full-fledged HTTP reverse proxy, the Symfony HTTP reverse proxy (via the `HttpCache` class) adds some nice debug info as HTTP headers. That helps greatly in validating the cache headers we have set.

Check it on the homepage:

```
$ curl -s -I -X GET https://127.0.0.1:8000/
```

```
HTTP/2 200
age: 0
cache-control: public, s-maxage=3600
content-type: text/html; charset=UTF-8
date: Mon, 28 Oct 2019 08:11:57 GMT
x-content-digest:
en63cef7045fe418859d73668c2703fb1324fcc0d35b21d95369a9ed1aca48e73e
x-debug-token: 9eb25a
x-debug-token-link: https://127.0.0.1:8000/_profiler/9eb25a
x-robots-tag: noindex
x-symfony-cache: GET /: miss, store
content-length: 50978
```

For the very first request, the cache server tells you that it was a miss and that it performed a store to cache the response. Check the cache-control header to see the configured cache strategy.

For subsequent requests, the response is cached (the age has also been updated):

```
HTTP/2 200
age: 143
cache-control: public, s-maxage=3600
content-type: text/html; charset=UTF-8
date: Mon, 28 Oct 2019 08:11:57 GMT
x-content-digest:
en63cef7045fe418859d73668c2703fb1324fcc0d35b21d95369a9ed1aca48e73e
x-debug-token: 9eb25a
x-debug-token-link: https://127.0.0.1:8000/_profiler/9eb25a
x-robots-tag: noindex
x-symfony-cache: GET /: fresh
content-length: 50978
```

21.3 Avoiding SQL Requests with ESI

The TwigEventSubscriber listener injects a global variable in Twig with all conference objects. It does so for every single page of the website. It is probably a great target for optimization.

You won't add new conferences every day, so the code is querying the exact same data from the database over and over again.

We might want to cache the conference names and slugs with the Symfony Cache, but whenever possible I like to rely on the HTTP caching infrastructure.

When you want to cache a fragment of a page, move it outside of the current HTTP request by creating a *sub-request*. *ESI* is a perfect match for this use case. An ESI is a way to embed the result of an HTTP request into another.

Create a controller that only returns the HTML fragment that displays the conferences:

```
--- a/src/Controller/ConferenceController.php
+++ b/src/Controller/ConferenceController.php
@@ -45,6 +45,16 @@ class ConferenceController extends AbstractController
         return $response;
     }

+    /**
+     * @Route("/conference_header", name="conference_header")
+     */
+    public function conferenceHeader(ConferenceRepository
$conferenceRepository)
+    {
+        return new Response($this->twig->render('conference/
header.html.twig', [
+            'conferences' => $conferenceRepository->findAll(),
+        ]));
+    }
+
     /**
      * @Route("/conference/{slug}", name="conference")
      */
```

Create the corresponding template:

```
templates/conference/header.html.twig
<ul>
    {% for conference in conferences %}
        <li><a href="{{ path('conference', { slug: conference.slug }) }}">{{
conference }}</a></li>
    {% endfor %}
</ul>
```

Hit `/conference_header` to check that everything works fine.

Time to reveal the trick! Update the Twig layout to call the controller we have just created:

```
--- a/templates/base.html.twig
+++ b/templates/base.html.twig
@@ -8,11 +8,7 @@
     <body>
         <header>
             <h1><a href="{{ path('homepage') }}">Guestbook</a></h1>
-            <ul>
-                {% for conference in conferences %}
-                    <li><a href="{{ path('conference', { slug: conference.slug })
```

```
}}">{{ conference }}</a></li>
-            {% endfor %}
-            </ul>
+            {{ render(path('conference_header')) }}
             <hr />
         </header>
         {% block body %}{% endblock %}
```

And *voilà*. Refresh the page and the website is still displaying the same.

 Use the "Request / Response" Symfony profiler panel to learn more about the main request and its sub-requests.

Now, every time you hit a page in the browser, two HTTP requests are executed, one for the header and one for the main page. You have made performance worse. Congratulations!

The conference header HTTP call is currently done internally by Symfony, so no HTTP round-trip is involved. This also means that there is no way to benefit from HTTP cache headers.

Convert the call to a "real" HTTP one by using an ESI.

First, enable ESI support:

```
--- a/config/packages/framework.yaml
+++ b/config/packages/framework.yaml
@@ -10,7 +10,7 @@ framework:
         cookie_secure: auto
         cookie_samesite: lax

-    #esi: true
+    esi: true
     #fragments: true
     php_errors:
         log: true
```

Then, use **render_esi** instead of **render**:

```
--- a/templates/base.html.twig
+++ b/templates/base.html.twig
@@ -8,7 +8,7 @@
     <body>
         <header>
             <h1><a href="{{ path('homepage') }}">Guestbook</a></h1>
-            {{ render(path('conference_header')) }}
+            {{ render_esi(path('conference_header')) }}
             <hr />
         </header>
         {% block body %}{% endblock %}
```

If Symfony detects a reverse proxy that knows how to deal with ESIs, it enables support automatically (if not, it falls back to render the sub-request synchronously).

As the Symfony reverse proxy does support ESIs, let's check its logs (remove the cache first - see "Purging" below):

```
$ curl -s -I -X GET https://127.0.0.1:8000/
```

```
HTTP/2 200
age: 0
cache-control: must-revalidate, no-cache, private
content-type: text/html; charset=UTF-8
date: Mon, 28 Oct 2019 08:20:05 GMT
expires: Mon, 28 Oct 2019 08:20:05 GMT
x-content-digest:
en4dd846a34dcd757eb9fd277f43220effd28c00e4117bed41af7f85700eb07f2c
x-debug-token: 719a83
x-debug-token-link: https://127.0.0.1:8000/_profiler/719a83
x-robots-tag: noindex
x-symfony-cache: GET /: miss, store; GET /conference_header: miss
content-length: 50978
```

Refresh a few times: the / response is cached and the /conference_header one is not. We have achieved something great: having the whole page in the cache but still having one part dynamic.

This is not what we want though. Cache the header page for an hour, independently of everything else:

```
--- a/src/Controller/ConferenceController.php
+++ b/src/Controller/ConferenceController.php
@@ -50,9 +50,12 @@ class ConferenceController extends AbstractController
     */
    public function conferenceHeader(ConferenceRepository
$conferenceRepository)
    {
-        return new Response($this->twig->render('conference/
header.html.twig', [
+        $response = new Response($this->twig->render('conference/
header.html.twig', [
            'conferences' => $conferenceRepository->findAll(),
        ]));
+        $response->setSharedMaxAge(3600);
+
+        return $response;
    }

    /**
```

Cache is now enabled for both requests:

```
$ curl -s -I -X GET https://127.0.0.1:8000/
```

```
HTTP/2 200
age: 613
cache-control: public, s-maxage=3600
content-type: text/html; charset=UTF-8
date: Mon, 28 Oct 2019 07:31:24 GMT
x-content-digest:
en15216b0803c7851d3d07071473c9f6a3a3360c6a83ccb0e550b35d5bc484bbd2
x-debug-token: cfb0e9
x-debug-token-link: https://127.0.0.1:8000/_profiler/cfb0e9
x-robots-tag: noindex
x-symfony-cache: GET /: fresh; GET /conference_header: fresh
content-length: 50978
```

The x-symfony-cache header contains two elements: the main / request
and a sub-request (the conference_header ESI). Both are in the cache
(fresh).

The cache strategy can be different from the main page and its ESIs. If we
have an "about" page, we might want to store it for a week in the cache,
and still have the header be updated every hour.

Remove the listener as we don't need it anymore:

```
$ rm src/EventSubscriber/TwigEventSubscriber.php
```

21.4 Purging the HTTP Cache for Testing

Testing the website in a browser or via automated tests becomes a little
bit more difficult with a caching layer.

You can manually remove all the HTTP cache by removing the var/
cache/dev/http_cache/ directory:

```
$ rm -rf var/cache/dev/http_cache/
```

This strategy does not work well if you only want to invalidate some
URLs or if you want to integrate cache invalidation in your functional
tests. Let's add a small, admin only, HTTP endpoint to invalidate some
URLs:

```
--- a/src/Controller/AdminController.php
+++ b/src/Controller/AdminController.php
@@ -6,8 +6,10 @@ use App\Entity\Comment;
 use App\Message\CommentMessage;
```

```
  use Doctrine\ORM\EntityManagerInterface;
  use Symfony\Bundle\FrameworkBundle\Controller\AbstractController;
+use Symfony\Bundle\FrameworkBundle\HttpCache\HttpCache;
  use Symfony\Component\HttpFoundation\Request;
  use Symfony\Component\HttpFoundation\Response;
+use Symfony\Component\HttpKernel\KernelInterface;
  use Symfony\Component\Messenger\MessageBusInterface;
  use Symfony\Component\Routing\Annotation\Route;
  use Symfony\Component\Workflow\Registry;
@@ -54,4 +56,19 @@ class AdminController extends AbstractController
            'comment' => $comment,
        ]);
    }
+
+    /**
+     * @Route("/admin/http-cache/{uri<.*>}", methods={"PURGE"})
+     */
+    public function purgeHttpCache(KernelInterface $kernel, Request $request,
string $uri)
+    {
+        if ('prod' === $kernel->getEnvironment()) {
+            return new Response('KO', 400);
+        }
+
+        $store = (new class($kernel) extends HttpCache {})->getStore();
+        $store->purge($request->getSchemeAndHttpHost().'/'.$uri);
+
+        return new Response('Done');
+    }
 }
```

The new controller has been restricted to the PURGE HTTP method. This
method is not in the HTTP standard, but it is widely used to invalidate
caches.

By default, route parameters cannot contain / as it separates URL
segments. You can override this restriction for the last route parameter,
like uri, by setting your own requirement pattern (.*).

The way we get the HttpCache instance can also look a bit strange; we are
using an anonymous class as accessing the "real" one is not possible. The
HttpCache instance wraps the real kernel, which is unaware of the cache
layer as it should be.

Invalidate the homepage and the conference header via the following
cURL calls:

```
$ curl -I -X PURGE -u admin:admin `symfony var:export
SYMFONY_DEFAULT_ROUTE_URL`/admin/http-cache/
$ curl -I -X PURGE -u admin:admin `symfony var:export
SYMFONY_DEFAULT_ROUTE_URL`/admin/http-cache/conference_header
```

The symfony var:export SYMFONY_DEFAULT_ROUTE_URL sub-command returns the current URL of the local web server.

 The controller does not have a route name as it will never be referenced in the code.

21.5 Grouping similar Routes with a Prefix

The two routes in the admin controller have the same /admin prefix. Instead of repeating it on all routes, refactor the routes to configure the prefix on the class itself:

```
--- a/src/Controller/AdminController.php
+++ b/src/Controller/AdminController.php
@@ -15,6 +15,9 @@ use Symfony\Component\Routing\Annotation\Route;
 use Symfony\Component\Workflow\Registry;
 use Twig\Environment;

+/**
+ * @Route("/admin")
+ */
 class AdminController extends AbstractController
 {
     private $twig;
@@ -29,7 +32,7 @@ class AdminController extends AbstractController
     }

     /**
-     * @Route("/admin/comment/review/{id}", name="review_comment")
+     * @Route("/comment/review/{id}", name="review_comment")
      */
     public function reviewComment(Request $request, Comment $comment,
Registry $registry)
     {
@@ -58,7 +61,7 @@ class AdminController extends AbstractController
     }

     /**
-     * @Route("/admin/http-cache/{uri<.*>}", methods={"PURGE"})
+     * @Route("/http-cache/{uri<.*>}", methods={"PURGE"})
      */
     public function flushHttpCache(KernelInterface $kernel, Request $request,
string $uri)
     {
```

21.6 Caching CPU/Memory Intensive Operations

We don't have CPU or memory-intensive algorithms on the website. To talk about *local caches*, let's create a command that displays the current step we are working on (to be more precise, the Git tag name attached to the current Git commit).

The Symfony Process component allows you to run a command and get the result back (standard and error output); install it:

```
$ symfony composer req process
```

Implement the command:

src/Command/StepInfoCommand.php
```php
namespace App\Command;

use Symfony\Component\Console\Command\Command;
use Symfony\Component\Console\Input\InputInterface;
use Symfony\Component\Console\Output\OutputInterface;
use Symfony\Component\Process\Process;

class StepInfoCommand extends Command
{
    protected static $defaultName = 'app:step:info';

    protected function execute(InputInterface $input, OutputInterface $output): int
    {
        $process = new Process(['git', 'tag', '-l', '--points-at', 'HEAD']);
        $process->mustRun();
        $output->write($process->getOutput());

        return 0;
    }
}
```

 You could have used `make:command` to create the command:

```
$ symfony console make:command app:step:info
```

What if we want to cache the output for a few minutes? Use the Symfony Cache:

```
$ symfony composer req cache
```

And wrap the code with the cache logic:

```
--- a/src/Command/StepInfoCommand.php
+++ b/src/Command/StepInfoCommand.php
@@ -6,16 +6,31 @@ use Symfony\Component\Console\Command\Command;
 use Symfony\Component\Console\Input\InputInterface;
```

```
 use Symfony\Component\Console\Output\OutputInterface;
 use Symfony\Component\Process\Process;
+use Symfony\Contracts\Cache\CacheInterface;

 class StepInfoCommand extends Command
 {
     protected static $defaultName = 'app:step:info';

+    private $cache;
+
+    public function __construct(CacheInterface $cache)
+    {
+        $this->cache = $cache;
+
+        parent::__construct();
+    }
+
     protected function execute(InputInterface $input, OutputInterface
$output): int
     {
-        $process = new Process(['git', 'tag', '-l', '--points-at', 'HEAD']);
-        $process->mustRun();
-        $output->write($process->getOutput());
+        $step = $this->cache->get('app.current_step', function ($item) {
+            $process = new Process(['git', 'tag', '-l', '--points-at',
'HEAD']);
+            $process->mustRun();
+            $item->expiresAfter(30);
+
+            return $process->getOutput();
+        });
+        $output->writeln($step);

         return 0;
     }
 }
```

The process is now only called if the `app.current_step` item is not in the
cache.

21.7 Profiling and Comparing Performance

Never add cache blindly. Keep in mind that adding some cache adds a
layer of complexity. And as we are all very bad at guessing what will be
fast and what is slow, you might end up in a situation where the cache
makes your application slower.

Always measure the impact of adding a cache with a profiler tool like
Blackfire[2].

Refer to the step about "Performance" to learn more about how you can

---

2. https://blackfire.io/

use Blackfire to test your code before deploying.

21.8 Configuring a Reverse Proxy Cache on Production

Don't use the Symfony reverse proxy in production. Always prefer a reverse proxy like Varnish on your infrastructure or a commercial CDN.

Add Varnish to the SymfonyCloud services:

```
--- a/.symfony/services.yaml
+++ b/.symfony/services.yaml
@@ -7,3 +7,12 @@ queue:
     type: rabbitmq:3.5
     disk: 1024
     size: S
+
+varnish:
+    type: varnish:6.0
+    relationships:
+        application: 'app:http'
+    configuration:
+        vcl: !include
+            type: string
+            path: config.vcl
```

Use Varnish as the main entry point in the routes:

```
--- a/.symfony/routes.yaml
+++ b/.symfony/routes.yaml
@@ -1,2 +1,2 @@
-"https://{all}/": { type: upstream, upstream: "app:http" }
+"https://{all}/": { type: upstream, upstream: "varnish:http", cache: {
enabled: false } }
 "http://{all}/": { type: redirect, to: "https://{all}/" }
```

Finally, create a `config.vcl` file to configure Varnish:

.symfony/config.vcl
```
sub vcl_recv {
    set req.backend_hint = application.backend();
}
```

21.9 Enabling ESI Support on Varnish

ESI support on Varnish should be enabled explicitly for each request. To make it universal, Symfony uses the standard `Surrogate-Capability` and `Surrogate-Control` headers to negotiate ESI support:

```
sub vcl_recv {
    set req.backend_hint = application.backend();
    set req.http.Surrogate-Capability = "abc=ESI/1.0";
}

sub vcl_backend_response {
    if (beresp.http.Surrogate-Control ~ "ESI/1.0") {
        unset beresp.http.Surrogate-Control;
        set beresp.do_esi = true;
    }
}
```

21.10 Purging the Varnish Cache

Invalidating the cache in production should probably never be needed, except for emergency purposes and maybe on non-master branches. If you need to purge the cache often, it probably means that the caching strategy should be tweaked (by lowering the TTL or by using a validation strategy instead of an expiration one).

Anyway, let's see how to configure Varnish for cache invalidation:

```
--- a/.symfony/config.vcl
+++ b/.symfony/config.vcl
@@ -1,6 +1,13 @@
 sub vcl_recv {
     set req.backend_hint = application.backend();
     set req.http.Surrogate-Capability = "abc=ESI/1.0";
+
+    if (req.method == "PURGE") {
+        if (req.http.x-purge-token != "PURGE_NOW") {
+            return(synth(405));
+        }
+        return (purge);
+    }
 }

 sub vcl_backend_response {
```

In real life, you would probably restrict by IPs instead like described in the *Varnish docs*[3].

Purge some URLs now:

```
$ curl -X PURGE -H 'x-purge-token PURGE_NOW' `symfony env:urls --first`
$ curl -X PURGE -H 'x-purge-token PURGE_NOW' `symfony env:urls --
first`conference_header
```

---

3. https://varnish-cache.org/docs/trunk/users-guide/purging.html

The URLs looks a bit strange because the URLs returned by `env:urls` already ends with /.

 Going Further

- *Cloudflare*[4], the global cloud platform;
- *Varnish HTTP Cache docs*[5];
- *ESI specification*[6] and *ESI developer resources*[7];
- *HTTP cache validation model*[8];
- *HTTP Cache in SymfonyCloud*[9].

4. https://www.cloudflare.com
5. https://varnish-cache.org/docs/index.html
6. https://www.w3.org/TR/esi-lang
7. https://www.akamai.com/us/en/support/esi.jsp
8. https://symfony.com/doc/current/http_cache/validation.html
9. https://symfony.com/doc/master/cloud/cookbooks/cache.html

Step 22

Styling the User Interface with Webpack

We have spent no time on the design of the user interface. To style like a pro, we will use a modern stack, based on *Webpack*[1]. And to add a Symfony touch and ease its integration with the application, let's install *Webpack Encore*:

```
$ symfony composer req encore
```

A full Webpack environment has been created for you: `package.json` and `webpack.config.js` have been generated and contain good default configuration. Open `webpack.config.js`, it uses the Encore abstraction to configure Webpack.

The `package.json` file defines some nice commands that we will use all the time.

The `assets` directory contains the main entry points for the project assets: `css/app.css` and `js/app.js`.

---

1. https://webpack.js.org/

22.1 Using Sass

Instead of using plain CSS, let's switch to *Sass*[2]:

```
$ mv assets/css/app.css assets/css/app.scss
```

```
--- a/assets/js/app.js
+++ b/assets/js/app.js
@@ -6,7 +6,7 @@
  */

  // any CSS you import will output into a single css file (app.css in this
case)
-import '../css/app.css';
+import '../css/app.scss';

  // Need jQuery? Install it with "yarn add jquery", then uncomment to import
it.
  // import $ from 'jquery';
```

Install the Sass loader:

```
$ yarn add node-sass "sass-loader@^7.0.1" --dev
```

And enable the Sass loader in webpack:

```
--- a/webpack.config.js
+++ b/webpack.config.js
@@ -54,7 +54,7 @@ Encore
    })

    // enables Sass/SCSS support
-    //.enableSassLoader()
+    .enableSassLoader()

    // uncomment if you use TypeScript
    //.enableTypeScriptLoader()
```

How did I know which packages to install? If we had tried to build our assets without them, Encore would have given us a nice error message suggesting the `yarn add` command needed to install dependencies to load `.scss` files.

---

2. https://sass-lang.com/

22.2 Leveraging Bootstrap

To start with good defaults and build a responsive website, a CSS framework like *Bootstrap*[3] can go a long way. Install it as a package:

```
$ yarn add bootstrap jquery popper.js bs-custom-file-input --dev
```

Require Bootstrap in the CSS file (we have also cleaned up the file):

```
--- a/assets/css/app.scss
+++ b/assets/css/app.scss
@@ -1,3 +1 @@
-body {
-    background-color: lightgray;
-}
+@import '~bootstrap/scss/bootstrap';
```

Do the same for the JS file:

```
--- a/assets/js/app.js
+++ b/assets/js/app.js
@@ -7,8 +7,7 @@

 // any CSS you import will output into a single css file (app.css in this
case)
 import '../css/app.scss';
+import 'bootstrap';
+import bsCustomFileInput from 'bs-custom-file-input';

-// Need jQuery? Install it with "yarn add jquery", then uncomment to import
it.
-// import $ from 'jquery';
-
-console.log('Hello Webpack Encore! Edit me in assets/js/app.js');
+bsCustomFileInput.init();
```

The Symfony form system supports Bootstrap natively with a special theme, enable it:

config/packages/twig.yaml
```
twig:
    form_themes: ['bootstrap_4_layout.html.twig']
```

22.3 Styling the HTML

We are now ready to style the application. Download and expand the

---

3. https://getbootstrap.com/

archive at the root of the project:

```
$ php -r "copy('https://symfony.com/uploads/assets/guestbook.zip',
'guestbook.zip');"
$ unzip -o guestbook.zip
$ rm guestbook.zip
```

Have a look at the templates, you might learn a trick or two about Twig.

22.4 Building Assets

One major change when using Webpack is that CSS and JS files are not usable directly by the application. They need to be "compiled" first.

In development, compiling the assets can be done via the `encore dev` command:

```
$ symfony run yarn encore dev
```

Instead of executing the command each time there is a change, send it to the background and let it watch JS and CSS changes:

```
$ symfony run -d yarn encore dev --watch
```

Take the time to discover the visual changes. Have a look at the new design in a browser.

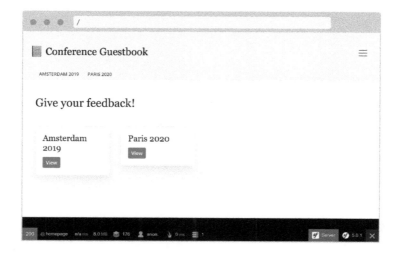

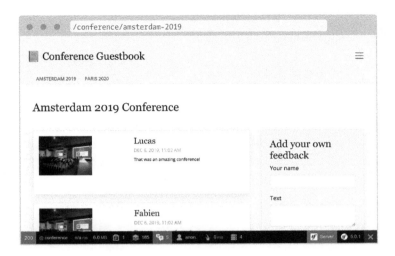

The generated login form is now styled as well as the Maker bundle uses Bootstrap CSS classes by default:

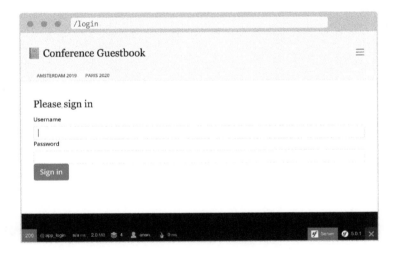

For production, SymfonyCloud automatically detects that you are using Encore and compiles the assets for you during the build phase.

Going Further

- *Webpack docs*[4];
- *Symfony Webpack Encore docs*[5];
- *SymfonyCasts Webpack Encore tutorial*[6].

---

4. https://webpack.js.org/concepts/
5. https://symfony.com/doc/current/frontend.html
6. https://symfonycasts.com/screencast/webpack-encore

Step 23
Resizing Images

On the conference page design, photos are constrained to a maximum size of 200 by 150 pixels. What about optimizing the images and reducing their size if the uploaded original is larger than the limits?

That is a perfect job that can be added to the comment workflow, probably just after the comment is validated and just before it is published.

Let's add a new **ready** state and an **optimize** transition:

```
--- a/config/packages/workflow.yaml
+++ b/config/packages/workflow.yaml
@@ -16,6 +16,7 @@ framework:
                - potential_spam
                - spam
                - rejected
+              - ready
                - published
            transitions:
                accept:
@@ -29,13 +30,16 @@ framework:
                    to:    spam
                publish:
                    from: potential_spam
-                  to:    published
+                  to:    ready
                reject:
                    from: potential_spam
                    to:    rejected
                publish_ham:
                    from: ham
```

```
-                 to:    published
+                 to:    ready
          reject_ham:
               from: ham
               to:    rejected
+         optimize:
+              from: ready
+              to:    published
```

Generate a visual representation of the new workflow configuration to validate that it describes what we want:

```
$ symfony console workflow:dump comment | dot -Tpng -o workflow.png
```

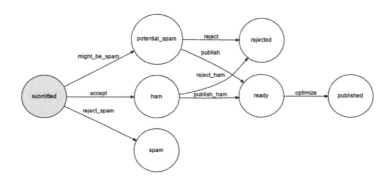

23.1 Optimizing Images with Imagine

Image optimizations will be done thanks to *GD*[1] (check that your local PHP installation has the GD extension enabled) and *Imagine*[2]:

```
$ symfony composer req imagine/imagine
```

Resizing an image can be done via the following service class:

src/ImageOptimizer.php
```
namespace App;

use Imagine\Gd\Imagine;
use Imagine\Image\Box;

class ImageOptimizer
```

---

1. https://libgd.github.io/
2. https://github.com/avalanche123/Imagine

```
{
    private const MAX_WIDTH = 200;
    private const MAX_HEIGHT = 150;

    private $imagine;

    public function __construct()
    {
        $this->imagine = new Imagine();
    }

    public function resize(string $filename): void
    {
        list($iwidth, $iheight) = getimagesize($filename);
        $ratio = $iwidth / $iheight;
        $width = self::MAX_WIDTH;
        $height = self::MAX_HEIGHT;
        if ($width / $height > $ratio) {
            $width = $height * $ratio;
        } else {
            $height = $width / $ratio;
        }

        $photo = $this->imagine->open($filename);
        $photo->resize(new Box($width, $height))->save($filename);
    }
}
```

After optimizing the photo, we store the new file in place of the original one. You might want to keep the original image around though.

23.2 Adding a new Step in the Workflow

Modify the workflow to handle the new state:

```
--- a/src/MessageHandler/CommentMessageHandler.php
+++ b/src/MessageHandler/CommentMessageHandler.php
@@ -2,6 +2,7 @@

 namespace App\MessageHandler;

+use App\ImageOptimizer;
 use App\Message\CommentMessage;
 use App\Repository\CommentRepository;
 use App\SpamChecker;
@@ -21,10 +22,12 @@ class CommentMessageHandler implements
MessageHandlerInterface
     private $bus;
     private $workflow;
     private $mailer;
+    private $imageOptimizer;
     private $adminEmail;
```

```
+      private $photoDir;
       private $logger;

-      public function __construct(EntityManagerInterface $entityManager,
SpamChecker $spamChecker, CommentRepository $commentRepository,
MessageBusInterface $bus, WorkflowInterface $commentStateMachine,
MailerInterface $mailer, string $adminEmail, LoggerInterface $logger = null)
+      public function __construct(EntityManagerInterface $entityManager,
SpamChecker $spamChecker, CommentRepository $commentRepository,
MessageBusInterface $bus, WorkflowInterface $commentStateMachine,
MailerInterface $mailer, ImageOptimizer $imageOptimizer, string $adminEmail,
string $photoDir, LoggerInterface $logger = null)
       {
           $this->entityManager = $entityManager;
           $this->spamChecker = $spamChecker;
@@ -32,7 +35,9 @@ class CommentMessageHandler implements
MessageHandlerInterface
           $this->bus = $bus;
           $this->workflow = $commentStateMachine;
           $this->mailer = $mailer;
+          $this->imageOptimizer = $imageOptimizer;
           $this->adminEmail = $adminEmail;
+          $this->photoDir = $photoDir;
           $this->logger = $logger;
       }

@@ -63,6 +68,12 @@ class CommentMessageHandler implements
MessageHandlerInterface
                   ->to($this->adminEmail)
                   ->context(['comment' => $comment])
               );
+          } elseif ($this->workflow->can($comment, 'optimize')) {
+              if ($comment->getPhotoFilename()) {
+                  $this->imageOptimizer->resize($this->photoDir.'/'.$comment-
>getPhotoFilename());
+              }
+              $this->workflow->apply($comment, 'optimize');
+              $this->entityManager->flush();
           } elseif ($this->logger) {
               $this->logger->debug('Dropping comment message', ['comment' =>
$comment->getId(), 'state' => $comment->getState()]);
           }
```

Note that **$photoDir** is automatically injected as we defined a container
bind on this variable name in a previous step:

config/packages/services.yaml
```yaml
services:
    _defaults:
        bind:
            $photoDir: "%kernel.project_dir%/public/uploads/photos"
```

23.3 Storing Uploaded Data in Production

We have already defined a special read-write directory for uploaded files in `.symfony.cloud.yaml`. But the mount is local. If we want the web container and the message consumer worker to be able to access the same mount, we need to create a *file service*:

```
--- a/.symfony/services.yaml
+++ b/.symfony/services.yaml
@@ -16,3 +16,7 @@ varnish:
        vcl: !include
            type: string
            path: config.vcl
+
+files:
+    type: network-storage:1.0
+    disk: 256
```

Use it for the photos upload directory:

```
--- a/.symfony.cloud.yaml
+++ b/.symfony.cloud.yaml
@@ -29,7 +29,7 @@ disk: 512

 mounts:
     "/var": { source: local, source_path: var }
-    "/public/uploads": { source: local, source_path: uploads }
+    "/public/uploads": { source: service, service: files, source_path:
uploads }

 hooks:
     build: |
```

This should be enough to make the feature work in production.

Step 24
Running Crons

Crons are useful to do maintenance tasks. Unlike workers, they run on a schedule for a short period of time.

24.1 Cleaning up Comments

Comments marked as spam or rejected by the admin are kept in the database as the admin might want to inspect them for a little while. But they should probably be removed after some time. Keeping them around for a week after their creation is probably enough.

Create some utility methods in the comment repository to find rejected comments, count them, and delete them:

```
--- a/src/Repository/CommentRepository.php
+++ b/src/Repository/CommentRepository.php
@@ -6,6 +6,7 @@ use App\Entity\Comment;
 use App\Entity\Conference;
 use Doctrine\Bundle\DoctrineBundle\Repository\ServiceEntityRepository;
 use Doctrine\Persistence\ManagerRegistry;
+use Doctrine\ORM\QueryBuilder;
 use Doctrine\ORM\Tools\Pagination\Paginator;

 /**
@@ -16,12 +17,37 @@ use Doctrine\ORM\Tools\Pagination\Paginator;
  */
 class CommentRepository extends ServiceEntityRepository
 {
+    private const DAYS_BEFORE_REJECTED_REMOVAL = 7;
```

```
 +
        public const PAGINATOR_PER_PAGE = 2;

        public function __construct(ManagerRegistry $registry)
        {
            parent::__construct($registry, Comment::class);
        }
 +
 +      public function countOldRejected(): int
 +      {
 +          return $this->getOldRejectedQueryBuilder()->select('COUNT(c.id)')-
>getQuery()->getSingleScalarResult();
 +      }
 +
 +      public function deleteOldRejected(): int
 +      {
 +          return $this->getOldRejectedQueryBuilder()->delete()->getQuery()-
>execute();
 +      }
 +
 +      private function getOldRejectedQueryBuilder(): QueryBuilder
 +      {
 +          return $this->createQueryBuilder('c')
 +              ->andWhere('c.state = :state_rejected or c.state = :state_spam')
 +              ->andWhere('c.createdAt < :date')
 +              ->setParameters([
 +                  'state_rejected' => 'rejected',
 +                  'state_spam' => 'spam',
 +                  'date' => new \DateTime(-self::DAYS_BEFORE_REJECTED_REMOVAL.'
days'),
 +              ])
 +          ;
 +      }

        public function getCommentPaginator(Conference $conference, int $offset):
Paginator
        {
```

 For more complex queries, it is sometimes useful to have a look at the generated SQL statements (they can be found in the logs and in the profiler for Web requests).

24.2 Using Class Constants, Container Parameters, and Environment Variables

7 days? We could have chosen another number, maybe 10 or 20. This number might evolve over time. We have decided to store it as a constant on the class, but we might have stored it as a parameter in the container, or we might have even defined it as an environment variable.

Here are some rules of thumb to decide which abstraction to use:

- If the value is sensitive (passwords, API tokens, ...), use the Symfony *secret storage* or a Vault;

- If the value is dynamic and you should be able to change it *without* re-deploying, use an *environment variable*;

- If the value can be different between environments, use a *container parameter*;

- For everything else, store the value in code, like in a *class constant*.

24.3 Creating a CLI Command

Removing the old comments is the perfect task for a cron job. It should be done on a regular basis, and a little delay does not have any major impact.

Create a CLI command named `app:comment:cleanup` by creating a `src/Command/CommentCleanupCommand.php` file:

src/Command/CommentCleanupCommand.php
```php
namespace App\Command;

use App\Repository\CommentRepository;
use Symfony\Component\Console\Command\Command;
use Symfony\Component\Console\Input\InputInterface;
use Symfony\Component\Console\Input\InputOption;
use Symfony\Component\Console\Output\OutputInterface;
use Symfony\Component\Console\Style\SymfonyStyle;

class CommentCleanupCommand extends Command
{
    private $commentRepository;

    protected static $defaultName = 'app:comment:cleanup';

    public function __construct(CommentRepository $commentRepository)
    {
        $this->commentRepository = $commentRepository;

        parent::__construct();
    }

    protected function configure()
    {
        $this
            ->setDescription('Deletes rejected and spam comments from the
database')
            ->addOption('dry-run', null, InputOption::VALUE_NONE, 'Dry run')
```

```
        ;
    }

    protected function execute(InputInterface $input, OutputInterface
$output): int
    {
        $io = new SymfonyStyle($input, $output);

        if ($input->getOption('dry-run')) {
            $io->note('Dry mode enabled');

            $count = $this->commentRepository->countOldRejected();
        } else {
            $count = $this->commentRepository->deleteOldRejected();
        }

        $io->success(sprintf('Deleted "%d" old rejected/spam comments.',
$count));

        return 0;
    }
}
```

All application commands are registered alongside Symfony built-in ones
and they are all accessible via symfony console. As the number of
available commands can be large, you should namespace them. By
convention, the application commands should be stored under the app
namespace. Add any number of sub-namespaces by separating them by
a colon (:).

A command gets the *input* (arguments and options passed to the
command) and you can use the *output* to write to the console.

Clean up the database by running the command:

```
$ symfony console app:comment:cleanup
```

24.4 Setting up a Cron on SymfonyCloud

One of the nice things about SymfonyCloud is that most of the
configuration is stored in one file: .symfony.cloud.yaml. The web
container, the workers, and the cron jobs are described together to help
maintenance:

```
--- a/.symfony.cloud.yaml
+++ b/.symfony.cloud.yaml
@@ -43,6 +43,15 @@ hooks:
```

```
    (>&2 symfony-deploy)
+crons:
+    comment_cleanup:
+        # Cleanup every night at 11.50 pm (UTC).
+        spec: '50 23 * * *'
+        cmd: |
+            if [ "$SYMFONY_BRANCH" = "master" ]; then
+                croncape symfony console app:comment:cleanup
+            fi
+
 workers:
     messages:
         commands:
```

The **crons** section defines all cron jobs. Each cron runs according to a **spec** schedule.

The **croncape** utility monitors the execution of the command and sends an email to the addresses defined in the **MAILTO** environment variable if the command returns any exit code different than **0**.

Configure the **MAILTO** environment variable:

```
$ symfony var:set MAILTO=ops@example.com
```

You can force a cron to run on your local machine:

```
$ symfony cron comment_cleanup
```

Note that crons are set up on all SymfonyCloud branches. If you don't want to run some on non-production environments, check the **$SYMFONY_BRANCH** environment variable:

```
if [ "$SYMFONY_BRANCH" = "master" ]; then
    croncape symfony app:invoices:send
fi
```

 Going Further

- *Cron/crontab syntax*[1];
- *Croncape repository*[2];
- *Symfony Console commands*[3];
- The *Symfony Console Cheat Sheet*[4].

1. https://en.wikipedia.org/wiki/Cron
2. https://github.com/symfonycorp/croncape
3. https://symfony.com/doc/current/console.html
4. https://github.com/andreia/symfony-cheat-sheets/blob/master/Symfony4/console_en_42.pdf

Step 25
Notifying by all Means

The Guestbook application gathers feedback about the conferences. But we are not great at giving feedback to our users.

As comments are moderated, they probably don't understand why their comments are not published instantly. They might even re-submit them thinking there was some technical problems. Giving them feedback after posting a comment would be great.

Also, we should probably ping them when their comment has been published. We ask for their email, so we'd better use it.

There are many ways to notify users. Email is the first medium that you might think about, but notifications in the web application is another one. We could even think about sending SMS messages, posting a message on Slack or Telegram. There are many options.

The Symfony Notifier Component implements many notification strategies:

```
$ symfony composer req notifier
```

25.1 Sending Web Application Notifications in the Browser

As a first step, let's notify the users that comments are moderated directly in the browser after their submission:

```
--- a/src/Controller/ConferenceController.php
+++ b/src/Controller/ConferenceController.php
@@ -14,6 +14,8 @@ use Symfony\Component\HttpFoundation\File\Exception\
FileException;
 use Symfony\Component\HttpFoundation\Request;
 use Symfony\Component\HttpFoundation\Response;
 use Symfony\Component\Messenger\MessageBusInterface;
+use Symfony\Component\Notifier\Notification\Notification;
+use Symfony\Component\Notifier\NotifierInterface;
 use Symfony\Component\Routing\Annotation\Route;
 use Symfony\Component\Workflow\Registry;
 use Twig\Environment;
@@ -60,7 +62,7 @@ class ConferenceController extends AbstractController
     /**
      * @Route("/conference/{slug}", name="conference")
      */
-    public function show(Request $request, Conference $conference,
CommentRepository $commentRepository, string $photoDir)
+    public function show(Request $request, Conference $conference,
CommentRepository $commentRepository, NotifierInterface $notifier, string
$photoDir)
     {
         $comment = new Comment();
         $form = $this->createForm(CommentFormType::class, $comment);
@@ -90,9 +92,15 @@ class ConferenceController extends AbstractController

             $this->bus->dispatch(new CommentMessage($comment->getId(),
$context));

+            $notifier->send(new Notification('Thank you for the feedback;
your comment will be posted after moderation.', ['browser']));
+
             return $this->redirectToRoute('conference', ['slug' =>
$conference->getSlug()]);
         }

+        if ($form->isSubmitted()) {
+            $notifier->send(new Notification('Can you check your submission?
There are some problems with it.', ['browser']));
+        }
+
         $offset = max(0, $request->query->getInt('offset', 0));
         $paginator = $commentRepository->getCommentPaginator($conference,
$offset);
```

The notifier *sends* a *notification* to *recipients* via a *channel*.

A notification has a subject, an optional content, and an importance.

A notification is sent on one or many channels depending on its importance. You can send urgent notifications by SMS and regular ones by email for instance.

For browser notifications, we don't have recipients.

The browser notification uses *flash messages* via the *notification* section. We need to display them by updating the conference template:

```
--- a/templates/conference/show.html.twig
+++ b/templates/conference/show.html.twig
@@ -3,6 +3,13 @@
 {% block title %}Conference Guestbook - {{ conference }}{% endblock %}

 {% block body %}
+    {% for message in app.flashes('notification') %}
+        <div class="alert alert-info alert-dismissible fade show">
+            {{ message }}
+            <button type="button" class="close" data-dismiss="alert" aria-
label="Close"><span aria-hidden="true">&times;</span></button>
+        </div>
+    {% endfor %}
+
     <h2 class="mb-5">
         {{ conference }} Conference
     </h2>
```

The users will now be notified that their submission is moderated:

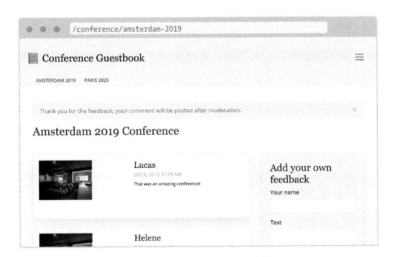

As an added bonus, we have a nice notification at the top of the website if there is a form error:

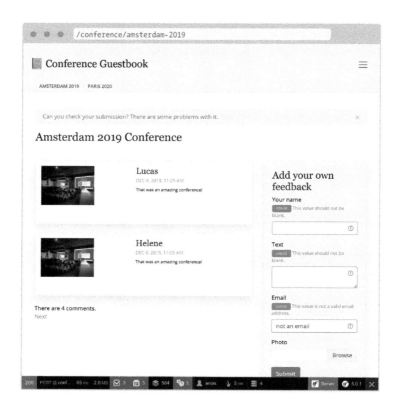

 Flash messages use the *HTTP session* system as a storage medium. The main consequence is that the HTTP cache is disabled as the session system must be started to check for messages.

This is the reason why we have added the flash messages snippet in the show.html.twig template and not in the base one as we would have lost HTTP cache for the homepage.

25.2 Notifying Admins by Email

Instead of sending an email via `MailerInterface` to notify the admin that a comment has just been posted, switch to use the Notifier component in the message handler:

```
--- a/src/MessageHandler/CommentMessageHandler.php
+++ b/src/MessageHandler/CommentMessageHandler.php
@@ -4,14 +4,14 @@ namespace App\MessageHandler;

 use App\ImageOptimizer;
```

```php
 use App\Message\CommentMessage;
+use App\Notification\CommentReviewNotification;
 use App\Repository\CommentRepository;
 use App\SpamChecker;
 use Doctrine\ORM\EntityManagerInterface;
 use Psr\Log\LoggerInterface;
-use Symfony\Bridge\Twig\Mime\NotificationEmail;
-use Symfony\Component\Mailer\MailerInterface;
 use Symfony\Component\Messenger\Handler\MessageHandlerInterface;
 use Symfony\Component\Messenger\MessageBusInterface;
+use Symfony\Component\Notifier\NotifierInterface;
 use Symfony\Component\Workflow\WorkflowInterface;

 class CommentMessageHandler implements MessageHandlerInterface
@@ -21,22 +21,20 @@ class CommentMessageHandler implements
MessageHandlerInterface
     private $commentRepository;
     private $bus;
     private $workflow;
-    private $mailer;
+    private $notifier;
     private $imageOptimizer;
-    private $adminEmail;
     private $photoDir;
     private $logger;

-    public function __construct(EntityManagerInterface $entityManager,
SpamChecker $spamChecker, CommentRepository $commentRepository,
MessageBusInterface $bus, WorkflowInterface $commentStateMachine,
MailerInterface $mailer, ImageOptimizer $imageOptimizer, string $adminEmail,
string $photoDir, LoggerInterface $logger = null)
+    public function __construct(EntityManagerInterface $entityManager,
SpamChecker $spamChecker, CommentRepository $commentRepository,
MessageBusInterface $bus, WorkflowInterface $commentStateMachine,
NotifierInterface $notifier, ImageOptimizer $imageOptimizer, string $photoDir,
LoggerInterface $logger = null)
     {
         $this->entityManager = $entityManager;
         $this->spamChecker = $spamChecker;
         $this->commentRepository = $commentRepository;
         $this->bus = $bus;
         $this->workflow = $commentStateMachine;
-        $this->mailer = $mailer;
+        $this->notifier = $notifier;
         $this->imageOptimizer = $imageOptimizer;
-        $this->adminEmail = $adminEmail;
         $this->photoDir = $photoDir;
         $this->logger = $logger;
     }
@@ -62,13 +60,7 @@ class CommentMessageHandler implements
MessageHandlerInterface

             $this->bus->dispatch($message);
         } elseif ($this->workflow->can($comment, 'publish') || $this-
>workflow->can($comment, 'publish_ham')) {
-            $this->mailer->send((new NotificationEmail())
-                ->subject('New comment posted')
```

```
-                    ->htmlTemplate('emails/comment_notification.html.twig')
-                    ->from($this->adminEmail)
-                    ->to($this->adminEmail)
-                    ->context(['comment' => $comment])
-                );
+                $this->notifier->send(new CommentReviewNotification($comment),
...$this->notifier->getAdminRecipients());
          } elseif ($this->workflow->can($comment, 'optimize')) {
              if ($comment->getPhotoFilename()) {
                  $this->imageOptimizer->resize($this->photoDir.'/'.$comment-
>getPhotoFilename());
```

The `getAdminRecipients()` method returns the admin recipients as configured in the notifier configuration; update it now to add your own email address:

```
--- a/config/packages/notifier.yaml
+++ b/config/packages/notifier.yaml
@@ -13,4 +13,4 @@ framework:
            medium: ['email']
            low: ['email']
        admin_recipients:
-            - { email: admin@example.com }
+            - { email:
"%env(string:default:default_admin_email:ADMIN_EMAIL)%" }
```

Now, create the `CommentReviewNotification` class:

src/Notification/CommentReviewNotification.php
```php
namespace App\Notification;

use App\Entity\Comment;
use Symfony\Component\Notifier\Message\EmailMessage;
use Symfony\Component\Notifier\Notification\EmailNotificationInterface;
use Symfony\Component\Notifier\Notification\Notification;
use Symfony\Component\Notifier\Recipient\Recipient;

class CommentReviewNotification extends Notification implements
EmailNotificationInterface
{
    private $comment;

    public function __construct(Comment $comment)
    {
        $this->comment = $comment;

        parent::__construct('New comment posted');
    }

    public function asEmailMessage(Recipient $recipient, string $transport =
null): ?EmailMessage
    {
        $message = EmailMessage::fromNotification($this, $recipient,
```

```
$transport);
        $message->getMessage()
            ->htmlTemplate('emails/comment_notification.html.twig')
            ->context(['comment' => $this->comment])
        ;

        return $message;
    }
}
```

The `asEmailMessage()` method from `EmailNotificationInterface` is optional, but it allows to customize the email.

One benefit of using the Notifier instead of the mailer directly to send emails is that it decouples the notification from the "channel" used for it. As you can see, nothing explicitly says that the notification should be sent by email.

Instead, the channel is configured in `config/packages/notifier.yaml` depending on the *importance* of the notification (`low` by default):

config/packages/notifier.yaml
```
framework:
notifier:
    channel_policy:
        # use chat/slack, chat/telegram, sms/twilio or sms/nexmo
        urgent: ['email']
        high: ['email']
        medium: ['email']
        low: ['email']
```

We have talked about the `browser` and the `email` channels. Let's see some fancier ones.

25.3 Chatting with Admins

Let's be honest, we all wait for positive feedback. Or at least constructive feedback. If someone posts a comment with words like "great" or "awesome", we might want to accept them faster than the others.

For such messages, we want to be alerted on an instant messaging system like Slack or Telegram in addition to the regular email.

Install Slack support for Symfony Notifier:

```
$ symfony composer req slack-notifier
```

To get started, compose the Slack DSN with a Slack access token and the Slack channel identifier where you want to send messages: `slack://ACCESS_TOKEN@default?channel=CHANNEL`.

As the access token is sensitive, store the Slack DSN in the secret store:

```
$ symfony console secrets:set SLACK_DSN
```

Do the same for production:

```
$ APP_ENV=prod symfony console secrets:set SLACK_DSN
```

Enable the chatter Slack support:

```
--- a/config/packages/notifier.yaml
+++ b/config/packages/notifier.yaml
@@ -1,7 +1,7 @@
 framework:
     notifier:
-        #chatter_transports:
-        #    slack: '%env(SLACK_DSN)%'
+        chatter_transports:
+            slack: '%env(SLACK_DSN)%'
         #    telegram: '%env(TELEGRAM_DSN)%'
         #texter_transports:
         #    twilio: '%env(TWILIO_DSN)%'
```

Update the Notification class to route messages depending on the comment text content (a simple regex will do the job):

```
--- a/src/Notification/CommentReviewNotification.php
+++ b/src/Notification/CommentReviewNotification.php
@@ -27,4 +27,15 @@ class CommentReviewNotification extends Notification
 implements EmailNotificationInterface
             ->context(['comment' => $this->comment])
         );
     }
+
+    public function getChannels(Recipient $recipient): array
+    {
+        if (preg_match('{\b(great|awesome)\b}i', $this->comment->getText())) {
+            return ['email', 'chat/slack'];
+        }
+
+        $this->importance(Notification::IMPORTANCE_LOW);
+
+        return ['email'];
+    }
 }
```

We have also changed the importance of "regular" comments as it slightly tweaks the design of the email.

And done! Submit a comment with "awesome" in the text, you should receive a message on Slack.

As for email, you can implement `ChatNotificationInterface` to override the default rendering of the Slack message:

```
--- a/src/Notification/CommentReviewNotification.php
+++ b/src/Notification/CommentReviewNotification.php
@@ -3,12 +3,17 @@
 namespace App\Notification;

 use App\Entity\Comment;
+use Symfony\Component\Notifier\Bridge\Slack\Block\SlackDividerBlock;
+use Symfony\Component\Notifier\Bridge\Slack\Block\SlackSectionBlock;
+use Symfony\Component\Notifier\Bridge\Slack\SlackOptions;
+use Symfony\Component\Notifier\Message\ChatMessage;
 use Symfony\Component\Notifier\Message\EmailMessage;
+use Symfony\Component\Notifier\Notification\ChatNotificationInterface;
 use Symfony\Component\Notifier\Notification\EmailNotificationInterface;
 use Symfony\Component\Notifier\Notification\Notification;
 use Symfony\Component\Notifier\Recipient\Recipient;

-class CommentReviewNotification extends Notification implements
EmailNotificationInterface
+class CommentReviewNotification extends Notification implements
EmailNotificationInterface, ChatNotificationInterface
 {
     private $comment;

@@ -30,6 +35,28 @@ class CommentReviewNotification extends Notification
implements EmailNotificatio
         return $message;
     }

+    public function asChatMessage(Recipient $recipient, string $transport =
null): ?ChatMessage
+    {
+        if ('slack' !== $transport) {
+            return null;
+        }
+
+        $message = ChatMessage::fromNotification($this, $recipient,
$transport);
+        $message->subject($this->getSubject());
+        $message->options((new SlackOptions())
+            ->iconEmoji('tada')
+            ->iconUrl('https://guestbook.example.com')
+            ->username('Guestbook')
+            ->block((new SlackSectionBlock())->text($this->getSubject()))
+            ->block(new SlackDividerBlock())
+            ->block((new SlackSectionBlock())
+                ->text(sprintf('%s (%s) says: %s', $this->comment-
>getAuthor(), $this->comment->getEmail(), $this->comment->getText()))
+            )
+        );
+
+        return $message;
+    }
```

```
+        public function getChannels(Recipient $recipient): array
         {
             if (preg_match('{\b(great|awesome)\b}i', $this->comment->getText())) {
```

It is better, but let's go one step further. Wouldn't it be awesome to be able to accept or reject a comment directly from Slack?

Change the notification to accept the review URL and add two buttons in the Slack message:

```
--- a/src/Notification/CommentReviewNotification.php
+++ b/src/Notification/CommentReviewNotification.php
@@ -3,6 +3,7 @@
 namespace App\Notification;

 use App\Entity\Comment;
+use Symfony\Component\Notifier\Bridge\Slack\Block\SlackActionsBlock;
 use Symfony\Component\Notifier\Bridge\Slack\Block\SlackDividerBlock;
 use Symfony\Component\Notifier\Bridge\Slack\Block\SlackSectionBlock;
 use Symfony\Component\Notifier\Bridge\Slack\SlackOptions;
@@ -16,10 +17,12 @@ use Symfony\Component\Notifier\Recipient\Recipient;
 class CommentReviewNotification extends Notification implements
 EmailNotificationInterface, ChatNotificationInterface
 {
     private $comment;
+    private $reviewUrl;

-    public function __construct(Comment $comment)
+    public function __construct(Comment $comment, string $reviewUrl)
     {
         $this->comment = $comment;
+        $this->reviewUrl = $reviewUrl;

         parent::__construct('New comment posted');
     }
@@ -52,6 +55,10 @@ class CommentReviewNotification extends Notification
 implements EmailNotificatio
             ->block((new SlackSectionBlock())
                 ->text(sprintf('%s (%s) says: %s', $this->comment-
>getAuthor(), $this->comment->getEmail(), $this->comment->getText()))
             )
+            ->block((new SlackActionsBlock())
+                ->button('Accept', $this->reviewUrl, 'primary')
+                ->button('Reject', $this->reviewUrl.'?reject=1', 'danger')
+            )
         );

         return $message;
```

It is now a matter of tracking changes backward. First, update the message handler to pass the review URL:

```
--- a/src/MessageHandler/CommentMessageHandler.php
+++ b/src/MessageHandler/CommentMessageHandler.php
@@ -60,7 +60,8 @@ class CommentMessageHandler implements
MessageHandlerInterface

                $this->bus->dispatch($message);
            } elseif ($this->workflow->can($comment, 'publish') || $this-
>workflow->can($comment, 'publish_ham')) {
-                $this->notifier->send(new CommentReviewNotification($comment),
...$this->notifier->getAdminRecipients());
+                $notification = new CommentReviewNotification($comment, $message-
>getReviewUrl());
+                $this->notifier->send($notification, ...$this->notifier-
>getAdminRecipients());
            } elseif ($this->workflow->can($comment, 'optimize')) {
                if ($comment->getPhotoFilename()) {
                    $this->imageOptimizer->resize($this->photoDir.'/'.$comment-
>getPhotoFilename());
```

As you can see, the review URL should be part of the comment message,
let's add it now:

```
--- a/src/Message/CommentMessage.php
+++ b/src/Message/CommentMessage.php
@@ -5,14 +5,21 @@ namespace App\Message;
 class CommentMessage
 {
     private $id;
+    private $reviewUrl;
     private $context;

-    public function __construct(int $id, array $context = [])
+    public function __construct(int $id, string $reviewUrl, array $context =
[])
     {
         $this->id = $id;
+        $this->reviewUrl = $reviewUrl;
         $this->context = $context;
     }

+    public function getReviewUrl(): string
+    {
+        return $this->reviewUrl;
+    }
+
     public function getId(): int
     {
         return $this->id;
```

Finally, update the controllers to generate the review URL and pass it in
the comment message constructor:

```
--- a/src/Controller/AdminController.php
```

```
+++ b/src/Controller/AdminController.php
@@ -12,6 +12,7 @@ use Symfony\Component\HttpFoundation\Response;
 use Symfony\Component\HttpKernel\KernelInterface;
 use Symfony\Component\Messenger\MessageBusInterface;
 use Symfony\Component\Routing\Annotation\Route;
+use Symfony\Component\Routing\Generator\UrlGeneratorInterface;
 use Symfony\Component\Workflow\Registry;
 use Twig\Environment;

@@ -51,7 +52,8 @@ class AdminController extends AbstractController
         $this->entityManager->flush();

         if ($accepted) {
-            $this->bus->dispatch(new CommentMessage($comment->getId()));
+            $reviewUrl = $this->generateUrl('review_comment', ['id' =>
$comment->getId()], UrlGeneratorInterface::ABSOLUTE_URL);
+            $this->bus->dispatch(new CommentMessage($comment->getId(),
$reviewUrl));
         }

         return $this->render('admin/review.html.twig', [
--- a/src/Controller/ConferenceController.php
+++ b/src/Controller/ConferenceController.php
@@ -17,6 +17,7 @@ use Symfony\Component\Messenger\MessageBusInterface;
 use Symfony\Component\Notifier\Notification\Notification;
 use Symfony\Component\Notifier\NotifierInterface;
 use Symfony\Component\Routing\Annotation\Route;
+use Symfony\Component\Routing\Generator\UrlGeneratorInterface;
 use Twig\Environment;

 class ConferenceController extends AbstractController
@@ -89,7 +90,8 @@ class ConferenceController extends AbstractController
                 'permalink' => $request->getUri(),
             ];

-            $this->bus->dispatch(new CommentMessage($comment->getId(),
$context));
+            $reviewUrl = $this->generateUrl('review_comment', ['id' =>
$comment->getId()], UrlGeneratorInterface::ABSOLUTE_URL);
+            $this->bus->dispatch(new CommentMessage($comment->getId(),
$reviewUrl, $context));

            $notifier->send(new Notification('Thank you for the feedback;
your comment will be posted after moderation.', ['browser']));
```

Code decoupling means changes in more places, but it makes it easier to test, reason about, and reuse.

Try again, the message should be in good shape now:

Guestbook `APP` 2:11 PM
New comment posted

Fabien (fan@sf.io) says: This conferences was really awesome. I will come back next year for sure. Keep up the good work.

Accept　Reject

25.4 Going Asynchronous across the Board

Let me explain a slight issue that we should fix. For each comment, we receive an email and a Slack message. If the Slack message errors (wrong channel id, wrong token, ...), the messenger message will be retried three times before being discarded. But as the email is sent first, we will receive 3 emails and no Slack messages. One way to fix it is to send Slack messages asynchronously like emails:

```
--- a/config/packages/messenger.yaml
+++ b/config/packages/messenger.yaml
@@ -20,3 +20,5 @@ framework:
            # Route your messages to the transports
            App\Message\CommentMessage: async
            Symfony\Component\Mailer\Messenger\SendEmailMessage: async
+           Symfony\Component\Notifier\Message\ChatMessage: async
+           Symfony\Component\Notifier\Message\SmsMessage: async
```

As soon as everything is asynchronous, messages become independent. We have also enabled asynchronous SMS messages in case you also want to be notified on your phone.

25.5 Notifying Users by Email

The last task is to notify users when their submission is approved. What about letting you implement that yourself?

Going Further

- *Symfony flash messages*[1].

---

1. https://symfony.com/doc/current/controller.html#flash-messages

Step 26
Exposing an API with API Platform

We have finished the implementation of the Guestbook website. To allow more usage of the data, what about exposing an API now? An API could be used by a mobile application to display all conferences, their comments, and maybe let attendees submit comments.

In this step, we are going to implement a read-only API.

26.1 Installing API Platform

Exposing an API by writing some code is possible, but if we want to use standards, we'd better use a solution that already takes care of the heavy lifting. A solution like API Platform:

```
$ symfony composer req api
```

26.2 Exposing an API for Conferences

A few annotations on the Conference class is all we need to configure the API:

```diff
--- a/src/Entity/Conference.php
+++ b/src/Entity/Conference.php
@@ -2,15 +2,24 @@

 namespace App\Entity;

+use ApiPlatform\Core\Annotation\ApiResource;
 use App\Repository\ConferenceRepository;
 use Doctrine\Common\Collections\ArrayCollection;
 use Doctrine\Common\Collections\Collection;
 use Doctrine\ORM\Mapping as ORM;
 use Symfony\Bridge\Doctrine\Validator\Constraints\UniqueEntity;
+use Symfony\Component\Serializer\Annotation\Groups;
 use Symfony\Component\String\Slugger\SluggerInterface;

 /**
  * @ORM\Entity(repositoryClass=ConferenceRepository::class)
  * @UniqueEntity("slug")
+ *
+ * @ApiResource(
+ *
collectionOperations={"get"={"normalization_context"={"groups"="conference:list"}}},
+ *
itemOperations={"get"={"normalization_context"={"groups"="conference:item"}}},
+ *     order={"year"="DESC", "city"="ASC"},
+ *     paginationEnabled=false
+ * )
  */
 class Conference
 {
@@ -18,21 +26,29 @@ class Conference
      * @ORM\Id()
      * @ORM\GeneratedValue()
      * @ORM\Column(type="integer")
+     *
+     * @Groups({"conference:list", "conference:item"})
      */
     private $id;

     /**
      * @ORM\Column(type="string", length=255)
+     *
+     * @Groups({"conference:list", "conference:item"})
      */
     private $city;

     /**
      * @ORM\Column(type="string", length=4)
+     *
+     * @Groups({"conference:list", "conference:item"})
      */
     private $year;

     /**
      * @ORM\Column(type="boolean")
+     *
+     * @Groups({"conference:list", "conference:item"})
```

```
    */
    private $isInternational;

@@ -43,6 +59,8 @@ class Conference

    /**
     * @ORM\Column(type="string", length=255, unique=true)
+    *
+    * @Groups({"conference:list", "conference:item"})
     */
    private $slug;
```

The main **@ApiResource** annotation configures the API for conferences. It restricts possible operations to **get** and configures various things: like which fields to display and how to order the conferences.

By default, the main entry point for the API is **/api** thanks to configuration from **config/routes/api_platform.yaml** that was added by the package's recipe.

A web interface allows you to interact with the API:

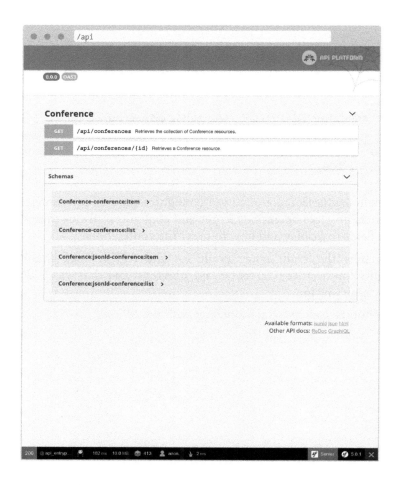

Use it to test the various possibilities:

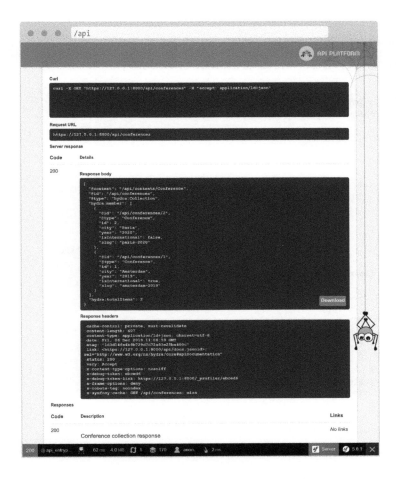

Imagine the time it would take to implement all of this from scratch!

26.3 Exposing an API for Comments

Do the same for comments:

```
--- a/src/Entity/Comment.php
+++ b/src/Entity/Comment.php
@@ -2,12 +2,25 @@

 namespace App\Entity;

+use ApiPlatform\Core\Annotation\ApiFilter;
+use ApiPlatform\Core\Annotation\ApiResource;
+use ApiPlatform\Core\Bridge\Doctrine\Orm\Filter\SearchFilter;
 use App\Repository\CommentRepository;
```

```
  use Doctrine\ORM\Mapping as ORM;
+use Symfony\Component\Serializer\Annotation\Groups;
  use Symfony\Component\Validator\Constraints as Assert;

 /**
  * @ORM\Entity(repositoryClass=CommentRepository::class)
  * @ORM\HasLifecycleCallbacks()
+ *
+ * @ApiResource(
+ *
collectionOperations={"get"={"normalization_context"={"groups"="comment:list"}}},
+ *
itemOperations={"get"={"normalization_context"={"groups"="comment:item"}}},
+ *      order={"createdAt"="DESC"},
+ *      paginationEnabled=false
+ * )
+ *
+ * @ApiFilter(SearchFilter::class, properties={"conference": "exact"})
  */
 class Comment
 {
@@ -15,18 +27,24 @@ class Comment
     * @ORM\Id()
     * @ORM\GeneratedValue()
     * @ORM\Column(type="integer")
+    *
+    * @Groups({"comment:list", "comment:item"})
     */
    private $id;

    /**
     * @ORM\Column(type="string", length=255)
     * @Assert\NotBlank
+    *
+    * @Groups({"comment:list", "comment:item"})
     */
    private $author;

    /**
     * @ORM\Column(type="text")
     * @Assert\NotBlank
+    *
+    * @Groups({"comment:list", "comment:item"})
     */
    private $text;

@@ -34,22 +52,30 @@ class Comment
     * @ORM\Column(type="string", length=255)
     * @Assert\NotBlank
     * @Assert\Email
+    *
+    * @Groups({"comment:list", "comment:item"})
     */
    private $email;

    /**
     * @ORM\Column(type="datetime")
```

```
+       *
+       * @Groups({"comment:list", "comment:item"})
        */
       private $createdAt;

       /**
        * @ORM\ManyToOne(targetEntity=Conference::class, inversedBy="comments")
        * @ORM\JoinColumn(nullable=false)
+       *
+       * @Groups({"comment:list", "comment:item"})
        */
       private $conference;

       /**
        * @ORM\Column(type="string", length=255, nullable=true)
+       *
+       * @Groups({"comment:list", "comment:item"})
        */
       private $photoFilename;
```

The same kind of annotations are used to configure the class.

26.4 Restricting Comments exposed by the API

By default, API Platform exposes all entries from the database. But for comments, only the published ones should be part of the API.

When you need to restrict the items returned by the API, create a service that implements `QueryCollectionExtensionInterface` to control the Doctrine query used for collections and/or `QueryItemExtensionInterface` to control items:

src/Api/FilterPublishedCommentQueryExtension.php
```php
namespace App\Api;

use ApiPlatform\Core\Bridge\Doctrine\Orm\Extension\
QueryCollectionExtensionInterface;
use ApiPlatform\Core\Bridge\Doctrine\Orm\Extension\QueryItemExtensionInterface;
use ApiPlatform\Core\Bridge\Doctrine\Orm\Util\QueryNameGeneratorInterface;
use App\Entity\Comment;
use Doctrine\ORM\QueryBuilder;

class FilterPublishedCommentQueryExtension implements
QueryCollectionExtensionInterface, QueryItemExtensionInterface
{
    public function applyToCollection(QueryBuilder $qb,
QueryNameGeneratorInterface $queryNameGenerator, string $resourceClass, string
$operationName = null)
    {
        if (Comment::class === $resourceClass) {
            $qb->andWhere(sprintf("%s.state = 'published'",
```

```
$qb->getRootAliases()[0]));
        }
    }

    public function applyToItem(QueryBuilder $qb, QueryNameGeneratorInterface
$queryNameGenerator, string $resourceClass, array $identifiers, string
$operationName = null, array $context = [])
    {
        if (Comment::class === $resourceClass) {
            $qb->andWhere(sprintf("%s.state = 'published'",
$qb->getRootAliases()[0]));
        }
    }
}
```

The query extension class applies its logic only for the Comment resource and modify the Doctrine query builder to only consider comments in the published state.

26.5 Configuring CORS

By default, the same-origin security policy of modern HTTP clients make calling the API from another domain forbidden. The CORS bundle, installed as part of composer req api, sends Cross-Origin Resource Sharing headers based on the CORS_ALLOW_ORIGIN environment variable.

By default, its value, defined in .env, allows HTTP requests from localhost and 127.0.0.1 on any port. That's exactly what we need as for the next step as we will create an SPA that will have its own web server that will call the API.

 Going Further

- *SymfonyCasts API Platform tutorial*[1];
- To enable the GraphQL support, run composer require webonyx/graphql-php, then browse to /api/graphql.

---

1. https://symfonycasts.com/screencast/api-platform

Step 27
Building an SPA

Most of the comments will be submitted during the conference where some people do not bring a laptop. But they probably have a smartphone. What about creating a mobile app to quickly check the conference comments?

One way to create such a mobile application is to build a Javascript Single Page Application (SPA). An SPA runs locally, can use local storage, can call a remote HTTP API, and can leverage service workers to create an almost native experience.

27.1 Creating the Application

To create the mobile application, we are going to use *Preact*[1] and **Symfony Encore**. **Preact** is a small and efficient foundation well-suited for the Guestbook SPA.

To make both the website and the SPA consistent, we are going to reuse the Sass stylesheets of the website for the mobile application.

Create the SPA application under the **spa** directory and copy the website stylesheets:

```
$ mkdir -p spa/src spa/public spa/assets/css
$ cp assets/css/*.scss spa/assets/css/
```

---

1. https://preactjs.com/

```
$ cd spa
```

 We have created a `public` directory as we will mainly interact with the SPA via a browser. We could have named it `build` if we only wanted to build a mobile application.

Initialize the `package.json` file (equivalent of the `composer.json` file for JavaScript):

```
$ yarn init -y
```

Now, add some required dependencies:

```
$ yarn add @symfony/webpack-encore @babel/core @babel/preset-env babel-preset-
preact preact html-webpack-plugin bootstrap
```

For good measure, add a .gitignore file:

.gitignore
```
/node_modules
/public
/yarn-error.log
# used later by Cordova
/app
```

The last configuration step is to create the Webpack Encore configuration:

webpack.config.js
```
const Encore = require('@symfony/webpack-encore');
const HtmlWebpackPlugin = require('html-webpack-plugin');

Encore
    .setOutputPath('public/')
    .setPublicPath('/')
    .cleanupOutputBeforeBuild()
    .addEntry('app', './src/app.js')
    .enablePreactPreset()
    .enableSingleRuntimeChunk()
    .addPlugin(new HtmlWebpackPlugin({ template: 'src/index.ejs',
alwaysWriteToDisk: true }))
;

module.exports = Encore.getWebpackConfig();
```

27.2 Creating the SPA Main Template

Time to create the initial template in which Preact will render the application:

src/index.ejs
```html
<!DOCTYPE html>
<html>
<head>
    <meta http-equiv="Content-Type" content="text/html; charset=utf-8" />
    <meta http-equiv="X-UA-Compatible" content="IE=edge" />
    <meta name="msapplication-tap-highlight" content="no" />
    <meta name="viewport" content="user-scalable=no, initial-scale=1, maximum-
scale=1, minimum-scale=1, width=device-width" />

    <title>Conference Guestbook application</title>
</head>
<body>
    <div id="app"></div>
</body>
</html>
```

The `<div>` tag is where the application will be rendered by JavaScript. Here is the first version of the code that renders the "Hello World" view:

src/app.js
```js
import {h, render} from 'preact';

function App() {
    return (
        <div>
            Hello world!
        </div>
    )
}

render(<App />, document.getElementById('app'));
```

The last line registers the `App()` function on the `#app` element of the HTML page.

Everything is now ready!

27.3 Running an SPA in the Browser

As this application is independent of the main website, we need to run another web server:

```
$ symfony server:start -d --passthru=index.html
```

The `--passthru` flag tells the web server to pass all HTTP requests to the `public/index.html` file (`public/` is the web server default web root directory). This page is managed by the Preact application and it gets the page to render via the "browser" history.

To compile the CSS **and the JavaScript** files, run `yarn`:

```
$ yarn encore dev
```

Open the SPA in a browser:

```
$ symfony open:local
```

And look at our hello world SPA:

27.4 Adding a Router to handle States

The SPA is currently not able to handle different pages. To implement several pages, we need a router, like for Symfony. We are going to use **preact-router**. It takes a URL as an input and matches a Preact component to display.

Install preact-router:

```
$ yarn add preact-router
```

Create a page for the homepage (a *Preact component*):

src/pages/home.js
```
import {h} from 'preact';

export default function Home() {
    return (
        <div>Home</div>
    );
};
```

And another for the conference page:

src/pages/conference.js
```
import {h} from 'preact';

export default function Conference() {
    return (
        <div>Conference</div>
    );
};
```

Replace the "Hello World" div with the Router component:

```
--- a/src/app.js
+++ b/src/app.js
@@ -1,9 +1,22 @@
 import {h, render} from 'preact';
+import {Router, Link} from 'preact-router';
+
+import Home from './pages/home';
+import Conference from './pages/conference';

 function App() {
     return (
         <div>
-            Hello world!
+            <header>
+                <Link href="/">Home</Link>
+                <br />
+                <Link href="/conference/amsterdam2019">Amsterdam 2019</Link>
+            </header>
+
+            <Router>
+                <Home path="/" />
+                <Conference path="/conference/:slug" />
+            </Router>
         </div>
     )
 }
```

Rebuild the application:

```
$ yarn encore dev
```

If you refresh the application in the browser, you can now click on the "Home" and conference links. Note that the browser URL and the back/forward buttons of your browser work as you would expect it.

27.5 Styling the SPA

As for the website, let's add the Sass loader:

```
$ yarn add node-sass "sass-loader@^7.0"
```

Enable the Sass loader in Webpack and add a reference to the stylesheet:

```
--- a/src/app.js
+++ b/src/app.js
@@ -1,3 +1,5 @@
+import '../assets/css/app.scss';
+
 import {h, render} from 'preact';
 import {Router, Link} from 'preact-router';

--- a/webpack.config.js
+++ b/webpack.config.js
@@ -7,6 +7,7 @@ Encore
     .cleanupOutputBeforeBuild()
     .addEntry('app', './src/app.js')
     .enablePreactPreset()
+    .enableSassLoader()
     .enableSingleRuntimeChunk()
     .addPlugin(new HtmlWebpackPlugin({ template: 'src/index.ejs',
alwaysWriteToDisk: true }))
 ;
```

We can now update the application to use the stylesheets:

```
--- a/src/app.js
+++ b/src/app.js
@@ -9,10 +9,20 @@ import Conference from './pages/conference';
 function App() {
     return (
         <div>
-            <header>
-                <Link href="/">Home</Link>
-                <br />
-                <Link href="/conference/amsterdam2019">Amsterdam 2019</Link>
+            <header className="header">
+                <nav className="navbar navbar-light bg-light">
```

```
+                    <div className="container">
+                        <Link className="navbar-brand mr-4 pr-2" href="/">
+                            &#128217; Guestbook
+                        </Link>
+                    </div>
+                </nav>
+
+                <nav className="bg-light border-bottom text-center">
+                    <Link className="nav-conference" href="/conference/
amsterdam2019">
+                        Amsterdam 2019
+                    </Link>
+                </nav>
            </header>

            <Router>
```

Rebuild the application once more:

```
$ yarn encore dev
```

You can now enjoy a fully styled SPA:

27.6 Fetching Data from the API

The Preact application structure is now finished: Preact Router handles
the page states - including the conference slug placeholder - and the main
application stylesheet is used to style the SPA.

To make the SPA dynamic, we need to fetch the data from the API via HTTP calls.

Configure Webpack to expose the API endpoint environment variable:

```
--- a/webpack.config.js
+++ b/webpack.config.js
@@ -1,3 +1,4 @@
+const webpack = require('webpack');
 const Encore = require('@symfony/webpack-encore');
 const HtmlWebpackPlugin = require('html-webpack-plugin');

@@ -10,6 +11,9 @@ Encore
     .enableSassLoader()
     .enableSingleRuntimeChunk()
     .addPlugin(new HtmlWebpackPlugin({ template: 'src/index.ejs',
alwaysWriteToDisk: true }))
+    .addPlugin(new webpack.DefinePlugin({
+        'ENV_API_ENDPOINT': JSON.stringify(process.env.API_ENDPOINT),
+    }))
 ;

 module.exports = Encore.getWebpackConfig();
```

The `API_ENDPOINT` environment variable should point to the web server of the website where we have the API endpoint under /api. We will configure it properly when we will run **yarn encore** soon.

Create an **api.js** file that abstracts data retrieval from the API:

src/api/api.js
```
function fetchCollection(path) {
    return fetch(ENV_API_ENDPOINT + path).then(resp => resp.json()).then(json
=> json['hydra:member']);
}

export function findConferences() {
    return fetchCollection('api/conferences');
}

export function findComments(conference) {
    return fetchCollection('api/comments?conference='+conference.id);
}
```

You can now adapt the header and home components:

```
--- a/src/app.js
+++ b/src/app.js
@@ -2,11 +2,23 @@ import '../assets/css/app.scss';

 import {h, render} from 'preact';
 import {Router, Link} from 'preact-router';
+import {useState, useEffect} from 'preact/hooks';
```

```
+import {findConferences} from './api/api';
 import Home from './pages/home';
 import Conference from './pages/conference';

 function App() {
+    const [conferences, setConferences] = useState(null);
+
+    useEffect(() => {
+        findConferences().then((conferences) => setConferences(conferences));
+    }, []);
+
+    if (conferences === null) {
+        return <div className="text-center pt-5">Loading...</div>;
+    }
+
     return (
         <div>
             <header className="header">
@@ -19,15 +31,17 @@ function App() {
                 </nav>

                 <nav className="bg-light border-bottom text-center">
-                    <Link className="nav-conference" href="/conference/
amsterdam2019">
-                        Amsterdam 2019
-                    </Link>
+                    {conferences.map((conference) => (
+                        <Link className="nav-conference"
href={'/conference/'+conference.slug}>
+                            {conference.city} {conference.year}
+                        </Link>
+                    ))}
                 </nav>
             </header>

             <Router>
-                <Home path="/" />
-                <Conference path="/conference/:slug" />
+                <Home path="/" conferences={conferences} />
+                <Conference path="/conference/:slug"
conferences={conferences} />
             </Router>
         </div>
     )
--- a/src/pages/home.js
+++ b/src/pages/home.js
@@ -1,7 +1,28 @@
 import {h} from 'preact';
+import {Link} from 'preact-router';
+
+export default function Home({conferences}) {
+    if (!conferences) {
+        return <div className="p-3 text-center">No conferences yet</div>;
+    }

-export default function Home() {
```

```
   return (
-          <div>Home</div>
+          <div className="p-3">
+              {conferences.map((conference)=> (
+                  <div className="card border shadow-sm lift mb-3">
+                      <div className="card-body">
+                          <div className="card-title">
+                              <h4 className="font-weight-light">
+                                  {conference.city} {conference.year}
+                              </h4>
+                          </div>
+
+                          <Link className="btn btn-sm btn-blue stretched-link"
href={'/conference/'+conference.slug}>
+                              View
+                          </Link>
+                      </div>
+                  </div>
+              ))}
+          </div>
   );
-};
+}
```

Finally, Preact Router is passing the "slug" placeholder to the Conference component as a property. Use it to display the proper conference and its comments, again using the API; and adapt the rendering to use the API data:

```
--- a/src/pages/conference.js
+++ b/src/pages/conference.js
@@ -1,7 +1,48 @@
 import {h} from 'preact';
+import {findComments} from '../api/api';
+import {useState, useEffect} from 'preact/hooks';
+
+function Comment({comments}) {
+    if (comments !== null && comments.length === 0) {
+        return <div className="text-center pt-4">No comments yet</div>;
+    }
+
+    if (!comments) {
+        return <div className="text-center pt-4">Loading...</div>;
+    }
+
+    return (
+        <div className="pt-4">
+            {comments.map(comment => (
+                <div className="shadow border rounded-lg p-3 mb-4">
+                    <div className="comment-img mr-3">
+                        {!comment.photoFilename ? '' : (
+                            <a href={ENV_API_ENDPOINT+'uploads/
photos/'+comment.photoFilename} target="_blank">
+                                <img src={ENV_API_ENDPOINT+'uploads/
```

```
 photos/'+comment.photoFilename} />
+                            </a>
+                        )}
+                    </div>
+
+                    <h5 className="font-weight-light mt-3
mb-0">{comment.author}</h5>
+                    <div className="comment-text">{comment.text}</div>
+                </div>
+            ))}
+        </div>
+    );
+}
+
+export default function Conference({conferences, slug}) {
+    const conference = conferences.find(conference => conference.slug ===
slug);
+    const [comments, setComments] = useState(null);
+
+    useEffect(() => {
+        findComments(conference).then(comments => setComments(comments));
+    }, [slug]);

-export default function Conference() {
     return (
-        <div>Conference</div>
+        <div className="p-3">
+            <h4>{conference.city} {conference.year}</h4>
+            <Comment comments={comments} />
+        </div>
     );
-};
+}
```

The SPA now needs to know the URL to our API, via the `API_ENDPOINT`
environment variable. Set it to the API web server URL (running in the
`..` directory):

```
$ API_ENDPOINT=`symfony var:export SYMFONY_DEFAULT_ROUTE_URL --dir=..` yarn
encore dev
```

You could also run in the background now:

```
$ API_ENDPOINT=`symfony var:export SYMFONY_DEFAULT_ROUTE_URL --dir=..` symfony
run -d --watch=webpack.config.js yarn encore dev --watch
```

And the application in the browser should now work properly:

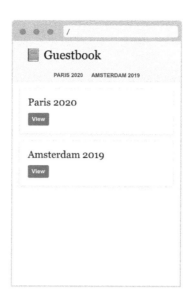

Wow! We now have a fully-functional, SPA with router and real data. We could organize the Preact app further if we want, but it is already working great.

27.7 Deploying the SPA in Production

SymfonyCloud allows to deploy multiple applications per project.

Adding another application can be done by creating a
.symfony.cloud.yaml file in any sub-directory. Create one under spa/
named spa:

.symfony.cloud.yaml

```yaml
name: spa

type: php:7.3
size: S
disk: 256

build:
    flavor: none

dependencies:
    nodejs:
        yarn: "*"

web:
    commands:
        start: sleep
    locations:
        "/":
            root: "public"
            index:
                - "index.html"
            scripts: false
            expires: 10m

hooks:
    build: |
        set -x -e

        curl -s https://get.symfony.com/cloud/configurator | (>&2 bash)
        yarn-install
        npm rebuild node-sass
        yarn encore prod
```

Edit the .symfony/routes.yaml file to route the spa. subdomain to the spa
application stored in the project root directory:

```
$ cd ../
```

```
--- a/.symfony/routes.yaml
+++ b/.symfony/routes.yaml
@@ -1,2 +1,5 @@
+"https://spa.{all}/": { type: upstream, upstream: "spa:http" }
+"http://spa.{all}/": { type: redirect, to: "https://spa.{all}/" }
+
 "https://{all}/": { type: upstream, upstream: "varnish:http", cache: {
enabled: false } }
 "http://{all}/": { type: redirect, to: "https://{all}/" }
```

27.8 Configuring CORS for the SPA

If you deploy the code now, it won't work as a browser would block the
API request. We need to explicitly allow the SPA to access the API. Get
the current domain name attached to your application:

```
$ symfony env:urls --first
```

Define the `CORS_ALLOW_ORIGIN` environment variable accordingly:

```
$ symfony var:set "CORS_ALLOW_ORIGIN=^`symfony env:urls --first | sed 's#/$##'
| sed 's#https://#https://spa.#'`$"
```

If your domain is `https://master-5szvwec-hzhac461b3a6o.eu.s5y.io/`, the
sed   calls   will   convert   it   to   `https://spa.master-5szvwec-`
`hzhac461b3a6o.eu.s5y.io`.

We also need to set the `API_ENDPOINT` environment variable:

```
$ symfony var:set API_ENDPOINT=`symfony env:urls --first`
```

Commit and deploy:

```
$ git add .
$ git commit -a -m'Add the SPA application'
$ symfony deploy
```

Access the SPA in a browser by specifying the application as a flag:

```
$ symfony open:remote --app=spa
```

27.9 Using Cordova to build a Smartphone Application

Apache Cordova is a tool that builds cross-platform smartphone
applications. And good news, it can use the SPA that we have just
created.

Let's install it:

```
$ cd spa
$ yarn global add cordova
```

You also need to install the Android SDK. This section only mentions Android, but Cordova works with all mobile platforms, including iOS.

Create the application directory structure:

```
$ cordova create app
```

And generate the Android application:

```
$ cd app
$ cordova platform add android
$ cd ..
```

That's all you need. You can now build the production files and move them to Cordova:

```
$ API_ENDPOINT=`symfony var:export SYMFONY_DEFAULT_ROUTE_URL --dir=..` yarn
encore production
$ rm -rf app/www
$ mkdir -p app/www
$ cp -R public/ app/www
```

Run the application on a smartphone or an emulator:

```
$ cordova run android
```

 Going Further

- *The official Preact website[2]*;
- *The official Cordova website[3].*

---

2. https://preactjs.com/
3. https://cordova.apache.org/

Step 28
Localizing an Application

With an international audience, Symfony has been able to handle internationalization (i18n) and localization (l10n) out of the box since like ever. Localizing an application is not just about translating the interface, it is also about plurals, date and currency formatting, URLs, and more.

28.1 Internationalizing URLs

The first step to internationalize the website is to internationalize the URLs. When translating a website interface, the URL should be different per locale to play nice with HTTP caches (never use the same URL and store the locale in the session).

Use the special `_locale` route parameter to reference the locale in routes:

```
--- a/src/Controller/ConferenceController.php
+++ b/src/Controller/ConferenceController.php
@@ -34,7 +34,7 @@ class ConferenceController extends AbstractController
     }

    /**
-     * @Route("/", name="homepage")
+     * @Route("/{_locale}/", name="homepage")
     */
    public function index(ConferenceRepository $conferenceRepository)
    {
```

On the homepage, the locale is now set internally depending on the URL; for instance, if you hit `/fr/`, `$request->getLocale()` returns `fr`.

As you will probably not be able to translate the content in all valid locales, restrict to the ones you want to support:

```
--- a/src/Controller/ConferenceController.php
+++ b/src/Controller/ConferenceController.php
@@ -34,7 +34,7 @@ class ConferenceController extends AbstractController
     }

     /**
-     * @Route("/{_locale}/", name="homepage")
+     * @Route("/{_locale<en|fr>}/", name="homepage")
     */
     public function index(ConferenceRepository $conferenceRepository)
     {
```

Each route parameter can be restricted by a regular expression inside `< >`. The `homepage` route now only matches when the `_locale` parameter is `en` or `fr`. Try hitting `/es/`, you should have a 404 as no route matches.

As we will use the same requirement in almost all routes, let's move it to a container parameter:

```
--- a/config/services.yaml
+++ b/config/services.yaml
@@ -7,6 +7,7 @@ parameters:
     default_admin_email: admin@example.com
     default_domain: '127.0.0.1'
     default_scheme: 'http'
+    app.supported_locales: 'en|fr'

    router.request_context.host:
'%env(default:default_domain:SYMFONY_DEFAULT_ROUTE_HOST)%'
    router.request_context.scheme:
'%env(default:default_domain:SYMFONY_DEFAULT_ROUTE_SCHEME)%'
--- a/src/Controller/ConferenceController.php
+++ b/src/Controller/ConferenceController.php
@@ -34,7 +34,7 @@ class ConferenceController extends AbstractController
     }

     /**
-     * @Route("/{_locale<en|fr>}/", name="homepage")
+     * @Route("/{_locale<%app.supported_locales%>}/", name="homepage")
     */
     public function index(ConferenceRepository $conferenceRepository)
     {
```

Adding a language can be done by updating the `app.supported_languages` parameter.

Add the same locale route prefix to the other URLs:

```
--- a/src/Controller/ConferenceController.php
+++ b/src/Controller/ConferenceController.php
@@ -47,7 +47,7 @@ class ConferenceController extends AbstractController
     }

     /**
-     * @Route("/conference_header", name="conference_header")
+     * @Route("/{_locale<%app.supported_locales%>}/conference_header",
name="conference_header")
     */
    public function conferenceHeader(ConferenceRepository
$conferenceRepository)
    {
@@ -60,7 +60,7 @@ class ConferenceController extends AbstractController
     }

     /**
-     * @Route("/conference/{slug}", name="conference")
+     * @Route("/{_locale<%app.supported_locales%>}/conference/{slug}",
name="conference")
     */
    public function show(Request $request, Conference $conference,
CommentRepository $commentRepository, NotifierInterface $notifier, string
$photoDir)
    {
```

We are almost done. We don't have a route that matches / anymore.
Let's add it back and make it redirect to /en/:

```
--- a/src/Controller/ConferenceController.php
+++ b/src/Controller/ConferenceController.php
@@ -33,6 +33,14 @@ class ConferenceController extends AbstractController
        $this->bus = $bus;
    }

+    /**
+     * @Route("/")
+     */
+    public function indexNoLocale()
+    {
+        return $this->redirectToRoute('homepage', ['_locale' => 'en']);
+    }
+
     /**
     * @Route("/{_locale<%app.supported_locales%>}/", name="homepage")
     */
```

Now that all main routes are locale aware, notice that generated URLs
on the pages take the current locale into account automatically.

28.2 Adding a Locale Switcher

To allow users to switch from the default en locale to another one, let's add a switcher in the header:

```
--- a/templates/base.html.twig
+++ b/templates/base.html.twig
@@ -34,6 +34,16 @@
                                    Admin
                        </a>
                    </li>
+<li class="nav-item dropdown">
+    <a class="nav-link dropdown-toggle" href="#" id="dropdown-language"
role="button"
+        data-toggle="dropdown" aria-haspopup="true" aria-expanded="false">
+        English
+    </a>
+    <div class="dropdown-menu dropdown-menu-right" aria-labelledby="dropdown-
language">
+        <a class="dropdown-item" href="{{ path('homepage', {_locale: 'en'})
}}">English</a>
+        <a class="dropdown-item" href="{{ path('homepage', {_locale: 'fr'})
}}">Français</a>
+    </div>
+</li>
                    </ul>
                </div>
            </div>
```

To switch to another locale, we explicitly pass the _locale route parameter to the path() function.

Update the template to display the current locale name instead of the hard-coded "English":

```
--- a/templates/base.html.twig
+++ b/templates/base.html.twig
@@ -37,7 +37,7 @@
 <li class="nav-item dropdown">
     <a class="nav-link dropdown-toggle" href="#" id="dropdown-language"
role="button"
        data-toggle="dropdown" aria-haspopup="true" aria-expanded="false">
-        English
+        {{ app.request.locale|locale_name(app.request.locale) }}
     </a>
     <div class="dropdown-menu dropdown-menu-right" aria-labelledby="dropdown-
language">
         <a class="dropdown-item" href="{{ path('homepage', {_locale: 'en'})
}}">English</a>
```

app is a global Twig variable that gives access to the current request. To convert the locale to a human readable string, we are using the locale_name Twig filter.

Depending on the locale, the locale name is not always capitalized. To capitalize sentences properly, we need a filter that is Unicode aware, as provided by the Symfony String component and its Twig implementation:

```
$ symfony composer req twig/string-extra
```

```
--- a/templates/base.html.twig
+++ b/templates/base.html.twig
@@ -37,7 +37,7 @@
 <li class="nav-item dropdown">
     <a class="nav-link dropdown-toggle" href="#" id="dropdown-language"
role="button"
         data-toggle="dropdown" aria-haspopup="true" aria-expanded="false">
-        {{ app.request.locale|locale_name(app.request.locale) }}
+        {{ app.request.locale|locale_name(app.request.locale)|u.title }}
     </a>
     <div class="dropdown-menu dropdown-menu-right" aria-labelledby="dropdown-
language">
         <a class="dropdown-item" href="{{ path('homepage', {_locale: 'en'})
}}">English</a>
```

You can now switch from French to English via the switcher and the whole interface adapts itself quite nicely:

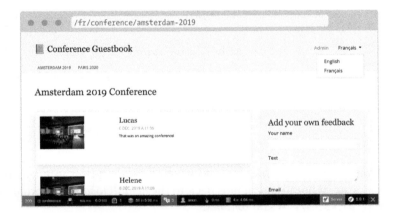

28.3 Translating the Interface

To start translating the website, we need to install the Symfony Translation component:

```
$ symfony composer req translation
```

Translating every single sentence on a large website can be tedious, but fortunately, we only have a handful of messages on our website. Let's start with all the sentences on the homepage:

```
--- a/templates/base.html.twig
+++ b/templates/base.html.twig
@@ -20,7 +20,7 @@
                <nav class="navbar navbar-expand-xl navbar-light bg-light">
                    <div class="container mt-4 mb-3">
                        <a class="navbar-brand mr-4 pr-2" href="{{
path('homepage') }}">
-                            &#128217; Conference Guestbook
+                            &#128217; {{ 'Conference Guestbook'|trans }}
                        </a>

                        <button class="navbar-toggler border-0" type="button"
data-toggle="collapse" data-target="#header-menu" aria-
controls="navbarSupportedContent" aria-expanded="false" aria-label="Afficher/
Cacher la navigation">
--- a/templates/conference/index.html.twig
+++ b/templates/conference/index.html.twig
@@ -4,7 +4,7 @@

 {% block body %}
    <h2 class="mb-5">
-        Give your feedback!
+        {{ 'Give your feedback!'|trans }}
    </h2>

    {% for row in conferences|batch(4) %}
@@ -21,7 +21,7 @@

                        <a href="{{ path('conference', { slug:
conference.slug }) }}"
                            class="btn btn-sm btn-blue stretched-link">
-                            View
+                            {{ 'View'|trans }}
                        </a>
                    </div>
                </div>
```

The **trans** Twig filter looks for a translation of the given input to the current locale. If not found, it falls back to the *default locale* as configured in **config/packages/translation.yaml**:

```
framework:
    default_locale: en
    translator:
        default_path: '%kernel.project_dir%/translations'
        fallbacks:
            - en
```

Notice that the web debug toolbar translation "tab" has turned red:

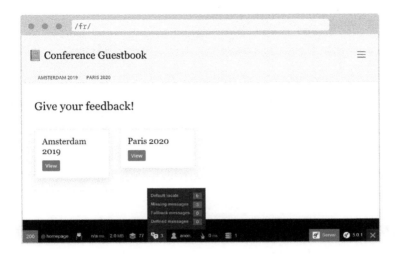

It tells us that 3 messages are not translated yet.

Click on the "tab" to list all messages for which Symfony did not find a translation:

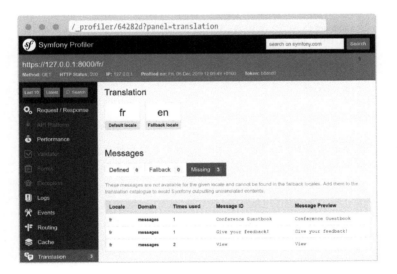

28.4 Providing Translations

As you might have seen in `config/packages/translation.yaml`, translations are stored under a `translations/` root directory, which has been created automatically for us.

Instead of creating the translation files by hand, use the

`translation:update` command:

```
$ symfony console translation:update fr --force --domain=messages
```

This command generates a translation file (`--force` flag) for the `fr` locale and the `messages` domain. The `messages` domain contains all **application** messages excluding the ones coming from Symfony itself like validation or security errors.

Edit the `translations/messages+intl-icu.fr.xlf` file and translate the messages in French. Don't speak French? Let me help you:

```
--- a/translations/messages+intl-icu.fr.xlf
+++ b/translations/messages+intl-icu.fr.xlf
@@ -7,15 +7,15 @@
     <body>
       <trans-unit id="LNAVleg" resname="Give your feedback!">
         <source>Give your feedback!</source>
-        <target>__Give your feedback!</target>
+        <target>Donnez votre avis !</target>
       </trans-unit>
       <trans-unit id="3Mg5pAF" resname="View">
         <source>View</source>
-        <target>__View</target>
+        <target>Sélectionner</target>
       </trans-unit>
       <trans-unit id="e0y4.6V" resname="Conference Guestbook">
         <source>Conference Guestbook</source>
-        <target>__Conference Guestbook</target>
+        <target>Livre d'Or pour Conferences</target>
       </trans-unit>
     </body>
   </file>
```

Note that we won't translate all templates, but feel free to do so:

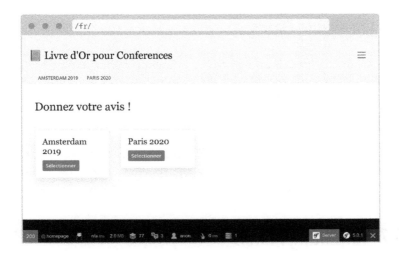

28.5 Translating Forms

Form labels are automatically displayed by Symfony via the translation system. Go to a conference page and click on the "Translation" tab of the web debug toolbar; you should see all labels ready for translation:

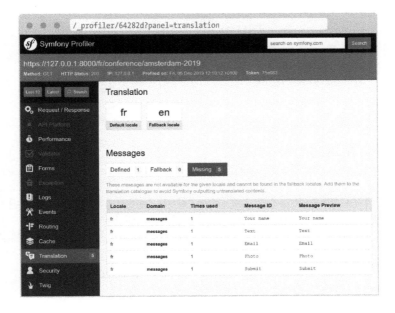

28.6 Localizing Dates

If you switch to French and go to a conference webpage that has some comments, you will notice that the comment dates are automatically localized. This works because we used the `format_datetime` Twig filter, which is locale-aware (`{{ comment.createdAt|format_datetime('medium', 'short') }}`).

The localization works for dates, times (`format_time`), currencies (`format_currency`), and numbers (`format_number`) in general (percents, durations, spell out, ...).

28.7 Translating Plurals

Managing plurals in translations is one usage of the more general problem of selecting a translation based on a condition.

On a conference page, we display the number of comments: `There are 2 comments`. For 1 comment, we display `There are 1 comments`, which is wrong. Modify the template to convert the sentence to a translatable message:

```
--- a/templates/conference/show.html.twig
+++ b/templates/conference/show.html.twig
@@ -37,7 +37,7 @@
                    </div>
                </div>
            {% endfor %}
-           <div>There are {{ comments|length }} comments.</div>
+           <div>{{ 'nb_of_comments'|trans({count: comments|length})
}}</div>
            {% if previous >= 0 %}
                <a href="{{ path('conference', { slug: conference.slug,
offset: previous }) }}">Previous</a>
            {% endif %}
```

For this message, we have used another translation strategy. Instead of keeping the English version in the template, we have replaced it with a unique identifier. That strategy works better for complex and large amount of text.

Update the translation file by adding the new message:

```
--- a/translations/messages+intl-icu.fr.xlf
+++ b/translations/messages+intl-icu.fr.xlf
@@ -17,6 +17,10 @@
        <source>View</source>
```

```
              <target>Sélectionner</target>
          </trans-unit>
+         <trans-unit id="Dg2dPd6" resname="nb_of_comments">
+            <source>nb_of_comments</source>
+            <target>{count, plural, =0 {Aucun commentaire.} =1 {1 commentaire.}
other {# commentaires.}}</target>
+         </trans-unit>
      </body>
    </file>
  </xliff>
```

We have not finished yet as we now need to provide the English translation. Create the `translations/messages+intl-icu.en.xlf` file:

translations/messages+intl-icu.en.xlf

```
<?xml version="1.0" encoding="utf-8"?>
<xliff xmlns="urn:oasis:names:tc:xliff:document:1.2" version="1.2">
  <file source-language="en" target-language="en" datatype="plaintext"
original="file.ext">
    <header>
      <tool tool-id="symfony" tool-name="Symfony"/>
    </header>
    <body>
      <trans-unit id="maMQz7W" resname="nb_of_comments">
        <source>nb of comments</source>
        <target>{count, plural, =0 {There are no comments.} one {There is one
comment.} other {There are # comments.}}</target>
      </trans-unit>
    </body>
  </file>
</xliff>
```

28.8 Updating Functional Tests

Don't forget to update the functional tests to take URLs and content changes into account:

```
--- a/tests/Controller/ConferenceControllerTest.php
+++ b/tests/Controller/ConferenceControllerTest.php
@@ -11,7 +11,7 @@ class ConferenceControllerTest extends WebTestCase
     public function testIndex()
     {
         $client = static::createClient();
-        $client->request('GET', '/');
+        $client->request('GET', '/en/');

         $this->assertResponseIsSuccessful();
         $this->assertSelectorTextContains('h2', 'Give your feedback');
@@ -20,7 +20,7 @@ class ConferenceControllerTest extends WebTestCase
     public function testCommentSubmission()
```

```
        {
            $client = static::createClient();
-           $client->request('GET', '/conference/amsterdam-2019');
+           $client->request('GET', '/en/conference/amsterdam-2019');
            $client->submitForm('Submit', [
                'comment_form[author]' => 'Fabien',
                'comment_form[text]' => 'Some feedback from an automated
functional test',
@@ -41,7 +41,7 @@ class ConferenceControllerTest extends WebTestCase
    public function testConferencePage()
        {
            $client = static::createClient();
-           $crawler = $client->request('GET', '/');
+           $crawler = $client->request('GET', '/en/');

            $this->assertCount(2, $crawler->filter('h4'));

@@ -50,6 +50,6 @@ class ConferenceControllerTest extends WebTestCase
            $this->assertPageTitleContains('Amsterdam');
            $this->assertResponseIsSuccessful();
            $this->assertSelectorTextContains('h2', 'Amsterdam 2019');
-           $this->assertSelectorExists('div:contains("There are 1 comments")');
+           $this->assertSelectorExists('div:contains("There is one comment")');
        }
    }
```

Going Further

- *Translating Messages using the ICU formatter*[1];
- *Using Twig translation filters*[2].

1. https://symfony.com/doc/current/translation/message_format.html
2. https://symfony.com/doc/current/translation/templates.html#translation-filters

Step 29
Managing Performance

> Premature optimization is the root of all evil.

Maybe you have already read this quotation before. But I like to cite it in full:

> We should forget about small efficiencies, say about 97% of the time: premature optimization is the root of all evil. Yet we should not pass up our opportunities in that critical 3%.
>
> —*Donald Knuth*

Even small performance improvements can make a difference, especially for e-commerce websites. Now that the guestbook application is ready for prime time, let's see how we can check its performance.

The best way to find performance optimizations is to use a *profiler*. The most popular option nowadays is *Blackfire*[1] (*full disclaimer*: I am also the founder of the Blackfire project).

---

1. https://blackfire.io

29.1 Introducing Blackfire

Blackfire is made of several parts:

- A *client* that triggers profiles (the Blackfire CLI tool or a browser extension for Google Chrome or Firefox);
- An *agent* that prepares and aggregates data before sending them to blackfire.io for display;
- A PHP extension (the *probe*) that instruments the PHP code.

To work with Blackfire, you first need to *sign up*[2].

Install Blackfire on your local machine by running the following quick installation script:

```
$ curl https://installer.blackfire.io/ | bash
```

This installer downloads the Blackfire CLI Tool and then installs the PHP probe (without enabling it) on all available PHP versions.

Enable the PHP probe for our project:

```
--- a/php.ini
+++ b/php.ini
@@ -6,3 +6,7 @@ max_execution_time=30
 session.use_strict_mode=On
 realpath_cache_ttl=3600
 zend.detect_unicode=Off
+
+[blackfire]
+# use php_blackfire.dll on Windows
+extension=blackfire.so
```

Restart the web server so that PHP can load Blackfire:

```
$ symfony server:stop
$ symfony server:start -d
```

The Blackfire CLI Tool needs to be configured with your personal **client** credentials (to store your project profiles under your personal account). Find them at the top of the Settings/Credentials *page*[3] and execute the following command by replacing the placeholders:

```
$ blackfire config --client-id=xxx --client-token=xxx
```

---

2. https://blackfire.io/signup
3. https://blackfire.io/my/settings/credentials

For full installation instructions, follow the official detailed installation guide. They are useful when installing Blackfire on a server.

29.2 Setting Up the Blackfire Agent on Docker

The last step is to add the Blackfire agent service in the Docker Compose stack:

```
--- a/docker-compose.yaml
+++ b/docker-compose.yaml
@@ -20,3 +20,8 @@ services:
     mailer:
         image: schickling/mailcatcher
         ports: [1025, 1080]
+
+    blackfire:
+        image: blackfire/blackfire
+        env_file: .env.local
+        ports: [8707]
```

To communicate with the server, you need to get your personal **server** credentials (these credentials identify where you want to store the profiles – you can create one per project); they can be found at the bottom of the `Settings/Credentials` *page*[4]. Store them in a local `.env.local` file:

```
BLACKFIRE_SERVER_ID=xxxxxxxx-xxxx-xxxx-xxxx-xxxxxxxxxxxx
BLACKFIRE_SERVER_TOKEN=xxxxxxxxxxxxxxxxxxxxxxxxxxxxxxxxxxxxxxxxxxxxxxxxxxxxxxxxxxxxxxxx
```

You can now launch the new container:

```
$ docker-compose stop
$ docker-compose up -d
```

29.3 Fixing a non-working Blackfire Installation

If you get an error while profiling, increase the Blackfire log level to get more information in the logs:

```
--- a/php.ini
```

---

4. https://blackfire.io/my/settings/credentials

```
+++ b/php.ini
@@ -10,3 +10,4 @@ zend.detect_unicode=Off
 [blackfire]
 # use php_blackfire.dll on Windows
 extension=blackfire.so
+blackfire.log_level=4
```

Restart the web server:

```
$ symfony server:stop
$ symfony server:start -d
```

And tail the logs:

```
$ symfony server:log
```

Profile again and check the log output.

29.4 Configuring Blackfire in Production

Blackfire is included by default in all SymfonyCloud projects.

Set up the *server* credentials as environment variables:

```
$ symfony var:set BLACKFIRE_SERVER_ID=xxxxxxxx-xxxx-xxxx-xxxx-xxxxxxxxxxxx
$ symfony var:set BLACKFIRE_SERVER_TOKEN=xxxxxxxxxxxxxxxxxxxxxxxxxxxxxxxx
```

And enable the PHP probe like any other PHP extension:

```
--- a/.symfony.cloud.yaml
+++ b/.symfony.cloud.yaml
@@ -4,6 +4,7 @@ type: php:7.3

 runtime:
    extensions:
+       - blackfire
        - xsl
        - amqp
        - redis
```

29.5 Configuring Varnish for Blackfire

Before you can deploy to start profiling, you need a way to bypass the Varnish HTTP cache. If not, Blackfire will never hit the PHP application. You are going to authorize the bypass of Varnish only for profiling requests coming from your local machine.

Find your current IP address:

```
$ curl https://ifconfig.me/
```

And use it to configure Varnish:

```
--- a/.symfony/config.vcl
+++ b/.symfony/config.vcl
@@ -1,3 +1,11 @@
+acl profile {
+    # Authorize the local IP address (replace with the IP found above)
+    "a.b.c.d";
+    # Authorize Blackfire servers
+    "46.51.168.2";
+    "54.75.240.245";
+}
+
 sub vcl_recv {
     set req.backend_hint = application.backend();
     set req.http.Surrogate-Capability = "abc=ESI/1.0";
@@ -8,6 +14,16 @@ sub vcl_recv {
         }
         return (purge);
     }
+
+    # Don't profile ESI requests
+    if (req.esi_level > 0) {
+        unset req.http.X-Blackfire-Query;
+    }
+
+    # Bypass Varnish when the profile request comes from a known IP
+    if (req.http.X-Blackfire-Query && client.ip ~ profile) {
+        return (pass);
+    }
 }

 sub vcl_backend_response {
```

You can now deploy.

29.6 Profiling Web Pages

You can profile traditional web pages from Firefox or Google Chrome via their *dedicated extensions*[5].

On your local machine, don't forget to disable the HTTP cache in public/index.php when profiling: if not, you will profile the Symfony HTTP cache layer instead of your own code:

---

5. https://blackfire.io/docs/integrations/browsers/index

```
--- a/public/index.php
+++ b/public/index.php
@@ -24,7 +24,7 @@ if ($trustedHosts = $_SERVER['TRUSTED_HOSTS'] ??
$_ENV['TRUSTED_HOSTS'] ?? false
 $kernel = new Kernel($_SERVER['APP_ENV'], (bool) $_SERVER['APP_DEBUG']);

 if ('dev' === $kernel->getEnvironment()) {
-    $kernel = new HttpCache($kernel);
+//    $kernel = new HttpCache($kernel);
 }

 $request = Request::createFromGlobals();
```

To get a better picture of the performance of your application in production, you should also profile the "production" environment. By default, your local environment is using the "development" environment, which adds a significant overhead (mainly to gather data for the web debug toolbar and the Symfony profiler).

Switching your local machine to the production environment can be done by changing the `APP_ENV` environment variable in the `.env.local` file:

```
APP_ENV=prod
```

Or you can use the **server:prod** command:

```
$ symfony server:prod
```

Don't forget to switch it back to dev when your profiling session ends:

```
$ symfony server:prod --off
```

29.7 Profiling API Resources

Profiling the API or the SPA is better done on the CLI via the Blackfire CLI Tool that you have installed previously:

```
$ blackfire curl `symfony var:export SYMFONY_DEFAULT_ROUTE_URL`api
```

The `blackfire curl` command accepts the exact same arguments and options as *cURL*[6].

---

6. https://curl.haxx.se/docs/manpage.html

29.8 Comparing Performance

In the step about "Cache", we added a cache layer to improve the performance of our code, but we did not check nor measure the performance impact of the change. As we are all very bad at guessing what will be fast and what is slow, you might end up in a situation where making some optimization actually makes your application slower.

You should always measure the impact of any optimization you do with a profiler. Blackfire makes it visually easier thanks to its *comparison feature*[7].

29.9 Writing Black Box Functional Tests

We have seen how to write functional tests with Symfony. Blackfire can be used to write browsing scenarios that can be run on demand via the *Blackfire player*[8]. Let's write a scenario that submits a new comment and validates it via the email link in development, and via the admin in production.

Create a .blackfire.yaml file with the following content:

.blackfire.yaml
```
scenarios: |
    #!blackfire-player

    group login
        visit url('/login')
        submit button("Sign in")
            param username "admin"
            param password "admin"
            expect status_code() == 302

    scenario
        name "Submit a comment on the Amsterdam conference page"
        include login
        visit url('/fr/conference/amsterdam-2019')
            expect status_code() == 200
        submit button("Submit")
            param comment_form[author] 'Fabien'
            param comment_form[email] 'me@example.com'
            param comment_form[text] 'Such a good conference!'
            param comment_form[photo] file(fake('image', '/tmp', 400, 300,
'cats'), 'awesome-cat.jpg')
            expect status_code() == 302
        follow
```

---

7. https://blackfire.io/docs/cookbooks/understanding-comparisons
8. https://blackfire.io/player

```
            expect status_code() == 200
            expect not(body() matches "/Such a good conference/")
            # Wait for the workflow to validate the submissions
            wait 5000
    when env != "prod"
        visit url(webmail_url ~ '/messages')
            expect status_code() == 200
            set message_ids json("[*].id")
        with message_id in message_ids
            visit url(webmail_url ~ '/messages/' ~ message_id ~ '.html')
                expect status_code() == 200
                set accept_url css("table a").first().attr("href")
            visit url(accept_url)
                # we don't check the status code as we can deal
                # with "old" messages which do not exist anymore
                # in the DB (would be a 404 then)
    when env == "prod"
        visit url('/admin/?entity=Comment&action=list')
            expect status_code() == 200
            set comment_ids css('table.table tbody tr').extract('data-id')
        with id in comment_ids
            visit url('/admin/comment/review/' ~ id)
                # we don't check the status code as we scan all comments,
                # including the ones already reviewed
    visit url('/fr/')
        wait 5000
    visit url('/fr/conference/amsterdam-2019')
        expect body() matches "/Such a good conference/"
```

Download the Blackfire player to be able to run the scenario locally:

```
$ curl -OLsS https://get.blackfire.io/blackfire-player.phar
$ chmod +x blackfire-player.phar
```

Run this scenario in development:

```
$ ./blackfire-player.phar run --endpoint=`symfony var:export
SYMFONY_DEFAULT_ROUTE_URL` .blackfire.yaml --variable "webmail_url=`symfony
var:export MAILER_WEB_URL 2>/dev/null`" --variable="env=dev"
```

Or in production:

```
$ ./blackfire-player.phar run --endpoint=`symfony env:urls --first`
.blackfire.yaml --variable "webmail_url=NONE" --variable="env=prod"
```

Blackfire scenarios can also trigger profiles for each request and run performance tests by adding the --blackfire flag.

29.10 Automating Performance Checks

Managing performance is not only about improving the performance of existing code, it is also about checking that no performance regressions are introduced.

The scenario written in the previous section can be run automatically in a Continuous Integration workflow or in production on a regular basis.

SymfonyCloud also allows to *run the scenarios*[9] whenever you create a new branch or deploy to production to check the performance of the new code automatically.

 Going Further

- *The Blackfire book: PHP Code Performance Explained*[10];
- *SymfonyCasts Blackfire tutorial*[11].

---

9. https://blackfire.io/docs/integrations/paas/symfonycloud#builds-level-enterprise
10. https://blackfire.io/book
11. https://symfonycasts.com/screencast/blackfire

Step 30
Discovering Symfony Internals

We have been using Symfony to develop a powerful application for quite a while now, but most of the code executed by the application comes from Symfony. A few hundred lines of code versus thousands of lines of code.

I like to understand how things work behind the scenes. And I have always been fascinated by tools that help me understand how things work. The first time I used a step by step debugger or the first time I discovered `ptrace` are magical memories.

Would you like to better understand how Symfony works? Time to dig into how Symfony makes your application tick. Instead of describing how Symfony handles an HTTP request from a theoretical perspective, which would be quite boring, we are going to use Blackfire to get some visual representations and use it to discover some more advanced topics.

30.1 Understanding Symfony Internals with Blackfire

You already know that all HTTP requests are served by a single entry point: the `public/index.php` file. But what happens next? How controllers are called?

Let's profile the English homepage in production with Blackfire via the Blackfire browser extension:

```
$ symfony remote:open
```

Or directly via the command line:

```
$ blackfire curl `symfony env:urls --first`en/
```

Go to the "Timeline" view of the profile, you should see something similar to the following:

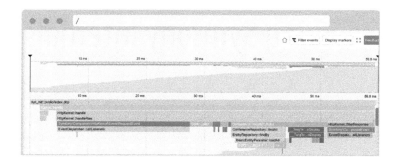

From the timeline, hover on the colored bars to have more information about each call; you will learn a lot about how Symfony works:

- The main entry point is `public/index.php`;
- The `Kernel::handle()` method handles the request;
- It calls the `HttpKernel` that dispatches some events;
- The first event is `RequestEvent`;
- The `ControllerResolver::getController()` method is called to determine which controller should be called for the incoming URL;
- The `ControllerResolver::getArguments()` method is called to determine which arguments to pass to the controller (the param converter is called);
- The `ConferenceController::index()` method is called and most of our code is executed by this call;
- The `ConferenceRepository::findAll()` method gets all conferences from the database (notice the connection to the database via `PDO::__construct()`);
- The `Twig\Environment::render()` method renders the template;
- The `ResponseEvent` and the `FinishRequestEvent` are dispatched, but

it looks like no listeners are actually registered as they seem to be really fast to execute.

The timeline is a great way to understand how some code works; which is very useful when you get a project developed by someone else.

Now, profile the same page from the local machine in the development environment:

```
$ blackfire curl `symfony var:export SYMFONY_DEFAULT_ROUTE_URL`en/
```

Open the profile. You should be redirected to the call graph view as the request was really quick and the timeline would be quite empty:

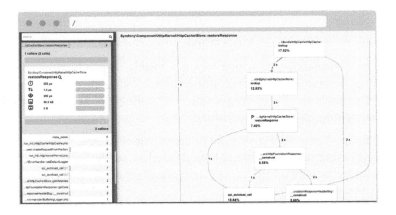

Do you understand what's going on? The HTTP cache is enabled and as such, we are profiling the Symfony HTTP cache layer. As the page is in the cache, `HttpCache\Store::restoreResponse()` is getting the HTTP response from its cache and the controller is never called.

Disable the cache layer in `public/index.php` as we did in the previous step and try again. You can immediately see that the profile looks very different:

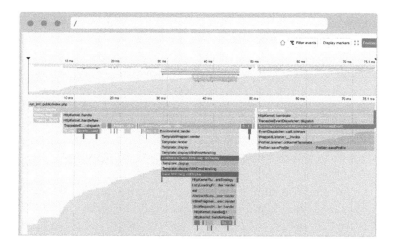

The main differences are the following:

- The TerminateEvent, which was not visible in production, takes a large percentage of the execution time; looking closer, you can see that this is the event responsible for storing the Symfony profiler data gathered during the request;

- Under the ConferenceController::index() call, notice the SubRequestHandler::handle() method that renders the ESI (that's why we have two calls to Profiler::saveProfile(), one for the main request and one for the ESI).

Explore the timeline to learn more; switch to the call graph view to have a different representation of the same data.

As we have just discovered, the code executed in development and production is quite different. The development environment is slower as the Symfony profiler tries to gather many data to ease debugging problems. This is why you should always profile with the production environment, even locally.

Some interesting experiments: profile an error page, profile the / page (which is a redirect), or an API resource. Each profile will tell you a bit more about how Symfony works, which class/methods are called, what is expensive to run and what is cheap.

30.2 Using the Blackfire Debug Addon

By default, Blackfire removes all method calls that are not significant enough to avoid having big payloads and big graphs. When using Blackfire as a debugging tool, it is better to keep all calls. This is provided by the debug addon.

From the command line, use the --debug flag:

```
$ blackfire --debug curl `symfony var:export SYMFONY_DEFAULT_ROUTE_URL`en/
$ blackfire --debug curl `symfony env:urls --first`en/
```

In production, you would see for instance the loading of a file named .env.local.php:

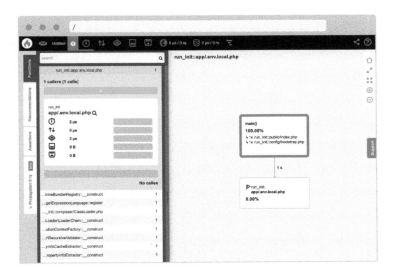

Where does it come from? SymfonyCloud does some optimizations when deploying a Symfony application like optimizing the Composer autoloader (--optimize-autoloader --apcu-autoloader --classmap-authoritative). It also optimizes environment variables defined in the .env file (to avoid parsing the file for every request) by generating the .env.local.php file:

```
$ symfony run composer dump-env prod
```

Blackfire is a very powerful tool that helps understand how code is executed by PHP. Improving performance is just one way to use a profiler.

Step 31
What's Next?

I hope you enjoyed the ride. I have tried to give you enough information to help you get started faster with your Symfony projects. We have barely scratched the surface of the Symfony world. Now, dive into the rest of the Symfony documentation to learn more about each feature we have discovered together.

Happy Symfony coding!

The more I live, the more I learn.
The more I learn, the more I realize, the less I know.
— *Michel Legrand*

Index

Performance Profiling and Testing for Symfony

Profile,
Test,
Fix,
Repeat.

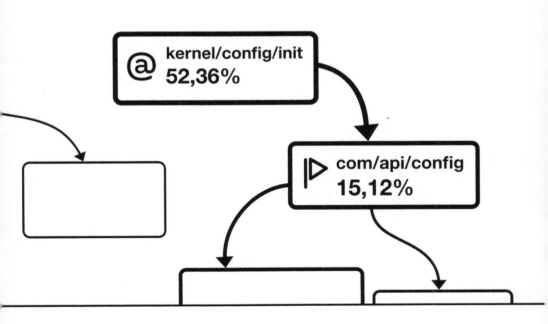